Letts
gets you through

ENGLISH LANGUAGE AND LITERATURE

EXAM PRACTICE WORKBOOK, WITH PRACTICE TEST PAPER

IAN KIRBY

About this Book

This exam practice workbook contains:

- topic-based questions for focused skills practice and to test your understanding of all the concepts on the GCSE 9-1 courses from AQA, Edexcel, OCR and WJEC Eduqas.
- practice papers to ensure you are thoroughly prepared for your GCSE exams.

Key features

> Practice papers to help you practise under exam conditions.

> Topic-based, exam-style questions to familiarise you with the type of questions you will get in the exams.

> Answers and mark scheme provided.

> If you need more help, turn to the matching pages in the Letts GCSE 9-1 English Language and Literature Revision Guide (ISBN 9780008318291).

> Mark your answers using the cut-out section at the back of the book.

Contents

Read Text 1, an extract from 'Auto Da Fay', the autobiography of the novelist Fay Weldon. Published in 2002, this extract describes an earthquake in New Zealand when her mother was still pregnant with Fay.

Text 1

When I was three months in the womb, in a period no doubt of nothing happening and nothing happening except a general warm all-pervasive dullness, an earthquake in Napier, New Zealand, had my mother Margaret running from the house with my two-year-old sister Jane in her arms. The year was 1931. My mother was twenty-three. Our house stayed upright but the grammar school opposite and the hospital down the road, both made of brick and not New Zealand's usual wood, collapsed. Everything else seemed made of matchsticks. My mother, in search of my father, one of the town's few doctors, ran past the grammar school and saw arms and legs sticking out of the rubble. But with a small child in your arms, what can you do for others? Everyone else was running too, some one way, some another: the ground was still shaking and changing and whether you were running into more danger or less how could you be sure? But still she ran.

Dr Frank Birkinshaw, my father, was too busy with the injured to take care of his young wife. He was a man of great charm, tall, well built, blue-eyed, adventurous and impetuous – at the time in his mid-thirties. Margaret was small, dark, fastidious and very, very pretty, with high cheekbones, big brown eyes and a gentle manner. The Birkinshaws were recent immigrants from England. He was from the North, had joined the army when he was sixteen, been invalided out of the trenches, and qualified as a doctor in the face of many obstacles. She was a bohemian from the softer South, an intellectual by birth, breeding, and temperament: her father a novelist, her mother a musician. She kept the company of Evelyn Waugh and his gang of friends, she was at home in literary soirées and in fashionable nightclubs, not in this harsh pioneering land. But she was also clever, determined and tough and failing to find my father, she left word for him, and by nightfall she and Jane had taken refuge in the tented city that went up overnight on the hills above Napier. The town was uninhabitable.

My mother was rescued from her makeshift tent by a sheep farmer and his wife, grateful patients of my father. They took her and little Jane to their homestead, where there was, my mother said, mutton for breakfast, mutton for dinner and mutton for tea. She helped around the farm, and cooked and ate the mutton with gratitude. I inherit this gift from her, I daresay, in that I do what is under my nose to be done, without too much lamentation.

Although the ground shook and trembled for weeks after the initial quake, meals continued to be served in the cookhouse, which had a tall brick chimney. My mother lived in fear of it collapsing and killing everyone inside, but no one would listen to her. She was dismissed as an alarmist. She was right, of course. There was another bad shock. 'I felt the trembling begin beneath my feet. I snatched Jane from her cot on the veranda and ran for open space but I was flung to the ground by what seemed a wave of dry land. I saw the hedge flick first one way and then the other. And then I watched the chimney fall into the cookhouse and destroy it. I always knew it would. I had already seen it happen.' As it fell out, dinner had finished just minutes before, and no one was killed, though for a time meals had to be eaten in the open air.

I have not inherited my mother's gift for prophecy: true, as you grow older you may begin to know what is going to happen next, but this can be put down to experience, not second sight. It is not a happy gift to have: because of it, for one thing, my mother never learned to drive, seeing too many scenarios of disaster ahead for comfort, too conscious of what might be going on over the brow of the hill. My father was very different: he was over-confident: he saw to the pleasures of the here-and-now and let the future go hang. I was born more like him than her, in this respect. She prophesied that it would land us both in trouble, and she was right.

1 Re-read the first paragraph. Choose four of the following statements that are true:
a) Fay was two years old when the earthquake took place. ☐
b) Fay's mother stopped to help everyone that she could. ☐
c) The earthquake took place in the city of Napier. ☐
d) Fay doesn't have any brothers or sisters. ☐
e) Fay's mother was 23 years old when the earthquake took place. ☐
f) Fay's mother's name is Margaret. ☐
g) The grammar school didn't collapse during the earthquake because it was brick-built. ☐
h) Fay's father was the local doctor. ☐ (4 marks)

2 Looking at the third paragraph, select one quotation that shows why the farmer looked after Fay's mother and one quotation that shows how she felt about this. (2 marks)

....

....

....

3 Looking at the second paragraph, summarise the differences between Fay's mother and father in your own words. (6 marks)

....

....

....

....

....

....

4 Referring to the second and fifth paragraphs, explain Fay's feelings about her mother. (6 marks)

....

....

....

....

....

....

5 How does Fay Weldon use language and structure to convey what the New Zealand earthquakes were like? (8 marks)
(Write your answer on a separate piece of paper.)

For more help on this topic, see Letts GCSE English Revision Guide pages 4–14.

Read Text 2, an extract from an essay 'Thoughts On Cheapness and My Aunt Charlotte', published in 1898 by the novelist H.G. Wells. In this extract, he describes the amount of good ornaments and furniture that his aunt used to keep, and wonders whether it's better to buy cheap things that will break rather than out-live you.

Text 2

All my Aunt Charlotte's furniture was thoroughly good, and most of it extremely uncomfortable; there was not a thing for a little boy to break and escape damnation in the household. Her china was the only thing with a touch of beauty in it – at least I remember nothing else – and each of her blessed plates was worth the happiness of a mortal for days together. I learned the value of thoroughly good things only too early. I knew the equivalent of a teacup to the very last scowl, and I have hated good, handsome property ever since. For my part I love cheap things, trashy things, things made of the commonest rubbish that money can possibly buy; things as vulgar as primroses, and as transitory as a morning's frost.

Think of all the advantages of a cheap possession – cheap and nasty, if you will – compared with some valuable substitute. Suppose you need this or that. "Get a good one," advises Aunt Charlotte; "one that will last." You do – and it does last. It lasts like a family curse. These great plain valuable things, as plain as good women, as complacently assured of their intrinsic worth – who does not know them? My Aunt Charlotte scarcely had a new thing in her life. Her mahogany was avuncular; her china remotely ancestral; her feather beds and her bedsteads! – they were haunted; the births, marriages, and deaths associated with the best one was the history of our race for three generations. There was more in her house than the tombstone rectitude of the chair-backs to remind me of the graveyard. I can still remember the sombre aisles of that house, the vault-like shadows, the magnificent window curtains that blotted out the windows. Life was too trivial for such things. She never knew she tired of them, but she did. That was the secret of her temper, I think; they engendered her sombre Calvinism, her perception of the trashy quality of human life. The pretence that they were the accessories to human life was too transparent. We were the accessories; we minded them for a little while, and then we passed away. They wore us out and cast us aside. We were the changing scenery; they were the actors who played on through the piece. It was even so with clothing. We buried my other maternal aunt – Aunt Adelaide – and wept, and partly forgot her; but her wonderful silk dresses – they would stand alone – still went rustling cheerfully about an ephemeral world.

All that offended my sense of proportion, my feeling of what is due to human life, even when I was a little boy. I want things of my own, things I can break without breaking my heart; and, since one can live but once, I want some change in my life – to have this kind of thing and then that. I never valued Aunt Charlotte's good old things until I sold them. They sold remarkably well: those chairs like nether millstones for the grinding away of men; the fragile china – an incessant anxiety until accident broke it, and the spell of it at the same time; those silver spoons, by virtue of which Aunt Charlotte went in fear of burglary for six-and-fifty years; the bed from which I alone of all my kindred had escaped; the wonderful old, erect, high-shouldered, silver-faced clock.

1 Re-read the last two paragraphs. Choose four of the following statements that are true:
   a) Aunt Charlotte believed in buying quality goods that would last. ☐
   b) Aunt Charlotte was always buying new things. ☐
   c) Wells found Aunt Charlotte's house warm and welcoming. ☐
   d) Wells also had an Aunt Adelaide. ☐
   e) Wells writes about Aunt Adelaide's dresses as if they were alive. ☐
   f) Wells eventually kept Aunt Charlotte's quality things rather than selling them. ☐

g) Aunt Charlotte was always worried about burglars. ☐

h) Wells says that he hates change. ☐ (4 marks)

2 Select two quotations from the second paragraph that show that Wells dislikes the idea that quality goods outlast their owners. (2 marks)

....

....

....

....

....

3 Looking at the last paragraph, summarise Wells's different thoughts about his Aunt Charlotte's 'good old things' in your own words. (4 marks)

....

....

....

....

....

4 Looking at the second paragraph, explain Wells's attitudes towards his Aunt Charlotte and her house. (6 marks)

....

....

....

....

....

....

....

5 Referring to the first paragraph, how does Wells use language and structure to convey his preference for cheap things over quality things? (8 marks)
(Write your answer on a separate piece of paper.)

6 Referring to Text 2 and Text 1, compare how the two writers convey their different feelings about members of their family. In your answer you should:
➤ compare their different feelings
➤ compare the methods they use to convey their different feelings
➤ support your ideas with quotations from both texts. (16 marks)
(Write your answer on a separate piece of paper.)

For more help on this topic, see Letts GCSE English Revision Guide pages 4–14.

Read Text 3, an article from *The Guardian* newspaper about kayaking in Australia. Written by Beverley Fearis, it was published in 2014.

Text 3

Melbourne in the moonlight: a nighttime kayak tour   (Beverley Fearis, The Guardian, Friday 4 April 2014)

One by one, balls of flames shot up from the towers like mini-infernos, lighting up the city skyline and casting a warm orange glow across the water below. We could hear the mighty whoosh each time the flames rose, followed by a hum of appreciation from the watching crowds lining the riverbank. The nightly fireball display in front of the Crown Casino has become a key feature of Melbourne's night scene, and we had the best seats in the house. Only thing was, we couldn't keep them still. That's the trouble with kayaks.

That morning we had cycled along the bank of the Yarra river, dodging office workers with their iPods and lattes, admiring the architecture and soaking up the city vibe. But now we were seeing Melbourne's hub from a whole different perspective – on a Moonlight Kayak tour, one of the city's more unusual sightseeing experiences. Under cover of darkness, we paddled silently up the Yarra like secret agents, passing under the bridges unseen. It was magical.

We had met at 7pm at Shed 2 of Victoria Harbour in the city's Docklands, like a smaller version of London's Docklands but catching up fast. Kent, our forever smiling (and ridiculously handsome) guide had introduced us to our ride, a two-seater fibreglass SeaBear sea kayak, and given us a quick but thorough briefing – life jackets, steering, paddling.

It was still light as we paddled off, and the low sun was glinting off the brilliant white super yachts lined up along the pontoons. At first, we stuck to the edge of the marina, getting used to our paddles and synchronising our strokes. The going was every bit as easy as Kent had promised. But then we changed direction and suddenly felt the force of the wind whipping across the water.

Warren, my fiancé, in the back, was in charge of steering with a foot pedal, but despite his best efforts we were being pushed towards the underside of a jetty. We had to use our paddles to help make the turn, really putting our backs into it to keep our distance. That was our only hairy moment, though, and we soon caught up with the others, in a sheltered corner of the marina.

Kent tied our kayaks to the jetty and left us chatting with our fellow urban adventurers. He returned a few minutes later with five portions of fish and chips, which we ate bobbing about in our kayaks, dipping our chips into the tartare sauce. Kent told us how he'd moved to Melbourne from Toronto for a marketing job but got sick of the corporate world. A keen kayaker, he'd come up with the idea of the Yarra tours. He does daytime trips too, but the moonlight tour has been the winner. "I think it's the fish and chips," he said, and to be fair they were a big part of the appeal.

Energy levels up, we headed off again, out into the mouth of the marina and past the Star Observation Wheel, Melbourne's answer to the London Eye. It opened in 2008 but closed 40 days later because of major structural defects (it had cracked in the heat). Dismantled and completely rebuilt, it opened again last December. At dusk it lights up in pretty neon colours.

As the sun set, we passed under the enormous Bolte Bridge, with its distinctive twin giant towers (purely aesthetic, Kent told us), then made a sharp left turn to head up the Yarra and into the heart of the city. The wind was in our favour now, so the paddling was easy and at times we let our blades rest and drifted along peacefully, taking it all in. Dusk turned to night and lights on the skyscrapers started to twinkle. As we cruised, Kent pointed out the landmarks, including the Eureka Skydeck, Melbourne's tallest highrise, named after a bloody rebellion during Victoria's 1854 gold rush. Next came the Webb Bridge, with its distinctive futuristic web tunnel for cyclists and pedestrians; and the Sandridge Bridge, with its large metal sculptures entitled The Travellers, representing the immigrants who arrived by train over the bridge from Station Pier. We slipped under the eerie undersides of these famous bridges, paddling through their shadowy arches, some of which were low enough to touch.

I had expected that we would be dodging pleasure cruisers and restaurant boats, waving to people in other boats (like you do when you're a tourist on water), but we had the river completely to ourselves. On either side of us the city night scene was hotting up, restaurants and bars buzzing, and here we were, on our moonlight urban kayak adventure, floating gently through the middle of it, trailing our fingers in the warm water, seeing it all, but unseen, from a vantage point like no other.

1 Re-read the second and third paragraphs. Choose four of the following statements that are true:
a) Fearis dislikes the city of Melbourne. ☐
b) Moonlight kayaking is quite unusual. ☐
c) Fearis enjoyed her kayaking experience. ☐
d) The guide was stern and miserable. ☐
e) They met at 7am before the sun came up. ☐
f) They all met up at Victoria Harbour. ☐
g) The kayaks were made from fibreglass. ☐
h) Fearis was scared as she didn't know what she was doing. ☐ (4 marks)

2 Select two quotations from the fourth paragraph that suggest Fearis enjoyed her kayaking experience. (2 marks)

....

....

....

3 Looking at the sixth paragraph, summarise Kent's reasons for setting up the moonlight kayaking tours. (4 marks)

....

....

....

....

....

....

4 Looking at the first paragraph, explain Fearis's attitudes toward the fireball display. (6 marks)
(Write your answer on a separate piece of paper.)

5 Referring to the last two paragraphs, how does Fearis use language and structure to convey the experience of moonlight kayaking? (8 marks)
(Write your answer on a separate piece of paper.)

For more help on this topic, see Letts GCSE English Revision Guide pages 4–14.

Read Text 4, a letter written by the novelist Charles Dickens in 1839 to his friend Thomas Mitton. Living in Exeter, Dickens writes to tell his friend about a cottage that he has decided to rent for his parents.

Text 4

New London Inn, Exeter
Wednesday Morning, March 6th, 1839.

Dear Tom,

Perhaps you have heard from Kate that I succeeded yesterday in the very first walk, and took a cottage at a place called Alphington, one mile from Exeter, which contains, on the ground-floor, a good parlour and kitchen, and above, a full-sized country drawing-room and three bedrooms; in the yard behind, coal-holes, fowl-houses, and meat-safes out of number; in the kitchen, a neat little range; in the other rooms, good stoves and cupboards; and all for twenty pounds a year, taxes included. There is a good garden at the side well stocked with cabbages, beans, onions, celery, and some flowers. The stock belonging to the landlady (who lives in the adjoining cottage), there was some question whether she was not entitled to half the produce, but I settled the point by paying five shillings, and becoming absolute master of the whole!

I do assure you that I am charmed with the place and the beauty of the country round about, though I have not seen it under very favourable circumstances, for it snowed when I was there this morning, and blew bitterly from the east yesterday. It is really delightful, and when the house is to rights and the furniture all in, I shall be quite sorry to leave it. I have had some few things second-hand, but I take it seventy pounds will be the mark, even taking this into consideration. I include in that estimate glass and crockery, garden tools, and such like little things. There is a spare bedroom of course. That I have furnished too.

I am on terms of the closest intimacy with Mrs. Samuell, the landlady, and her brother and sister-in-law, who have a little farm hard by. They are capital specimens of country folks, and I really think the old woman herself will be a great comfort to my mother. Coals are dear just now—twenty-six shillings a ton. They found me a boy to go two miles out and back again to order some this morning. I was debating in my mind whether I should give him eighteenpence or two shillings, when his fee was announced—twopence!

The house is on the high road to Plymouth, and, though in the very heart of Devonshire, there is as much long-stage and posting life as you would find in Piccadilly. The situation is charming. Meadows in front, an orchard running parallel to the garden hedge, richly-wooded hills closing in the prospect behind, and, away to the left, before a splendid view of the hill on which Exeter is situated, the cathedral towers rising up into the sky in the most picturesque manner possible. I don't think I ever saw so cheerful or pleasant a spot. The drawing-room is nearly, if not quite, as large as the outer room of my old chambers in Furnival's Inn. The paint and paper are new, and the place clean as the utmost excess of snowy cleanliness can be.

You will have heard perhaps that I wrote to my mother to come down to-morrow. There are so many things she can make comfortable at a much less expense than I could, that I thought it best. If I had not, I could not have returned on Monday, which I now hope to do, and to be in town at half-past eight.

Will you tell my father that if he could devise any means of bringing him down, I think it would be a great thing for him to have Dash, if it be only to keep down the trampers and beggars.

1 Re-read the last four paragraphs. Choose four of the following statements that are true:

a) Alphington is two miles away from Exeter ☐

b) Dickens doesn't really like Mrs Samuell, the landlady. ☐

c) Local coal is very cheap. ☐

d) The cottage is in Devonshire. ☐

e) The local area is beautiful. ☐

f) There is a view of a cathedral. ☐

g) The cottage needs a lot of cleaning. ☐

h) Dickens doesn't want his mother to see the cottage. ☐ (4 marks)

2 Select two quotations from the second paragraph that show that Dickens feels that the cottage has the potential to be even nicer in the future. (2 marks)

....

....

3 Looking at the fourth paragraph, summarise what we are told about the cottage's setting in your own words. (4 marks)

....

....

....

....

4 Looking at the third paragraph, explain Dickens's attitudes towards the locals he has met. (6 marks)

....

....

....

....

....

5 Referring to the first two paragraphs, how does Dickens use language and structure to convey his enthusiasm for the cottage he has rented for his parents? (8 marks)
(Write your answer on a separate piece of paper.)

6 Referring to Text 4 and Text 3, compare how the two writers convey their different feelings about people and places. In your answer you should:

➤ compare their different feelings

➤ compare the methods they use to convey their different feelings

➤ support your ideas with quotations from both texts. (16 marks)
(Write your answer on a separate piece of paper.)

For more help on this topic, see Letts GCSE English Revision Guide pages 4–14.

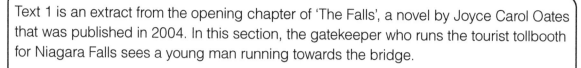

Text 1 is an extract from the opening chapter of 'The Falls', a novel by Joyce Carol Oates that was published in 2004. In this section, the gatekeeper who runs the tourist tollbooth for Niagara Falls sees a young man running towards the bridge.

Text 1

By this time the gatekeeper had decided to leave his tollbooth to follow the agitated man. Calling, "Mister! Hey mister!"—"Mister, wait!" He'd had experience with suicides in the past. More times than he wished to remember. He was a thirty-year veteran of The Falls tourist trade. He was in his early sixties, couldn't keep up with the younger man. Pleading, "Mister! Don't! God damn I'm begging you: *don't*!"

He should have dialled his emergency number, back in the tollbooth. Now it was too late to turn back.

Once on Goat Island the younger man didn't pause by the railing to gaze across the river at the Canadian shore, nor did he pause to contemplate the raging, tumultuous scene, as any normal tourist would do. He didn't pause even to wipe his streaming face, or brush his straggly hair out of his eyes. *Under the spell of The Falls. Nobody mortal was going to stop him.*

But you have to interfere, or try. Can't let a man – or a woman – commit suicide, the unforgiveable sin, before your staring eyes.

The gatekeeper, short of breath, light-headed, limped after the younger man shouting at him as he made his unerring way to the southern tip of the little island, Terrapin Point, above the Horseshoe Falls. The most treacherous corner of Goat Island, as it was the most beautiful and enthralling. Here the rapids go into a frenzy. White frothy churning water shooting up fifteen feet into the air. Hardly any visibility. The chaos of a nightmare. The Horseshoe Falls is a gigantic cataract a half-mile long at its crest, three thousand tons of water pouring over the Gorge each second. The air roars, shakes. The ground beneath your feet shakes. As if the very earth is beginning to come apart, disintegrate into particles, down to its molten centre. As if time has ceased. Time has exploded. As if you've come too near to the radiant, thrumming, mad heart of all being. Here, your veins, arteries, the minute precision and perfection of your nerves will be unstrung in an instant. Your brain, in which you reside, that one-of-a-kind repository of *you*, will be pounded into its chemical components: brain cells, molecules, atoms. Every shadow and echo of every memory erased.

Maybe that's the promise of The Falls? The secret?

Like we're sick of ourselves. Mankind. This is the way out, only a few have the vision.

Thirty yards from the younger man, the gatekeeper saw him place one foot on the lowest rung of the railing. A tentative foot, on the slippery wrought iron. But the man's hands gripped the top rung, both fists, tight,

"Don't do it! Mister! God damn—"

The gatekeeper's words were drowned out by The Falls. Flung back into his face like cold spit.

Near to collapsing, himself. This would be his last summer at Goat Island. His heart hurt, pounding to send oxygen to his stunned brain. And his lungs hurt, not only the stinging spray of the river but the strange metallic taste of the air of the industrial city sprawling east and north of The Falls, in which the gatekeeper had lived all his life. *You wear out. You see too much. Every breath hurts.*

The gatekeeper would afterward swear he'd seen the younger man make a gesture of farewell in the instant before he jumped: a mock salute, a salute of defiance, as a bright brash schoolboy might make to an elder, to provoke; yet a sincere farewell too, as you might make to a stranger, a witness to whom you mean no harm, whom you wish to absolve of the slightest shred of guilt he might feel, for allowing you to die when he might have saved you.

> And in the next instant the young man, who'd been commandeering the gatekeeper's exclusive attention, was simply – gone.
>
> In a heartbeat, gone. Over the Horseshoe Falls.

1 Look at the first paragraph. List four things about the gatekeeper. (4 marks)

....

....

....

....

2 Referring to the fifth paragraph, how has the writer used language to describe Niagara Falls? (8 marks)
(Write your answer on a separate piece of paper.)

3 You now need to think about the whole of the extract. This text is from the opening chapter of a novel. How has the writer structured the text to interest you as a reader?
You could write about:
➤ what the writer focused your attention on at the beginning
➤ how and why the writer alters this focus as the extract develops
➤ any other structural features that interest you. (8 marks)
(Write your answer on a separate piece of paper.)

4 A student, having read this extract said: 'The writer makes you feel so sorry for the old gatekeeper. He's desperate to stop the man but is totally helpless himself.' To what extent do you agree?
In your response, you should:
➤ write about your own impression of the gatekeeper
➤ evaluate how the writer has created these impressions
➤ support your opinions with quotations from the text. (20 marks)
(Write your answer on a separate piece of paper.)

5 Compare how Joyce Carol Oates and the author of your set modern text create atmosphere. Focus on the first four paragraphs of the extract and choose one atmospheric section from your modern text. You might consider:
➤ how descriptions of setting and events are used
➤ the effects of different characters' feelings. (20 marks)
(Write your answer on a separate piece of paper.)

6 Compare how Joyce Carol Oates and the author of your set modern text create interesting settings. Focus on the fifth paragraph of the extract and choose one interesting setting from your modern text. You might consider:
➤ how the settings are similar or different
➤ the different techniques used to make the settings interesting. (20 marks)
(Write your answer on a separate piece of paper.)

For more help on this topic, see Letts GCSE English Revision Guide pages 16–24.

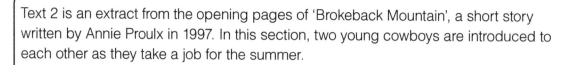

Text 2 is an extract from the opening pages of 'Brokeback Mountain', a short story written by Annie Proulx in 1997. In this section, two young cowboys are introduced to each other as they take a job for the summer.

Text 2

They were raised on small, poor ranches in opposite corners of the state, Jack Twist in Lightning Flat up on the Montana border, Ennis del Mar from around Sage, near the Utah line, both high school dropout country boys with no prospects, brought up to hard work and privation, both rough-mannered, rough-spoken, inured to the stoic life. Ennis, reared by his older brother and sister after their parents drove off the only curve on Dead Horse Road leaving them twenty-four dollars in cash and a two-mortgage ranch, applied at age fourteen for a hardship license that let him make the hour-long trip from the ranch to the high school. The pickup was old, no heater, one windshield wiper and bad tires; when the transmission went there was no money to fix it. He had wanted to be a sophomore, felt the word carried a kind of distinction, but the truck broke down short of it, pitching him directly into ranch work.

In 1963 when he met Jack Twist, Ennis was engaged to Alma Beers. Both Jack and Ennis claimed to be saving money for a small spread; in Ennis's case that meant a tobacco can with two five-dollar bills inside. That spring, hungry for any job, each had signed up with Farm and Ranch Employment – they came together on paper as herder and camp tender for the same sheep operation north of Signal. The summer range lay above the tree line on Forest Service land on Brokeback Mountain. It would be Jack Twist's second summer on the mountain, Ennis's first. Neither of them was twenty.

They shook hands in the choky little trailer office in front of a table littered with scribbled papers, a Bakelite ashtray brimming with stubs. The venetian blinds hung askew and admitted a triangle of white light, the shadow of the foreman's hand moving into it. Joe Aguirre, wavy hair the color of cigarette ash and parted down the middle, gave them his point of view.

"Forest Service got designated campsites on the allotments. Them camps can be a couple a miles from where we pasture the sheep. Bad predator loss, nobody near lookin after em at night. What I want, camp tender in the main camp where the Forest Service says, but the HERDER" – pointing at Jack with a chop of his hand – "pitch a pup tent on the q.t. with the sheep, out a sight, and he's goin a SLEEP there. Eat supper, breakfast in camp, but SLEEP WITH THE SHEEP, hunderd percent, NO FIRE, don't leave NO SIGN. Roll up that tent every mornin case Forest Service snoops around. Got the dogs, your .30-.30, sleep there. Last summer had goddamn near twenty-five percent loss. I don't want that again. YOU," he said to Ennis, taking in the ragged hair, the big nicked hands, the jeans torn, button-gaping shirt, "Fridays twelve noon be down at the bridge with your next week list and mules. Somebody with supplies'll be there in a pickup." He didn't ask if Ennis had a watch but took a cheap round ticker on a braided cord from a box on a high shelf, wound and set it, tossed it to him as if he weren't worth the reach. "TOMORROW MORNIN we'll truck you up the jump-off." Pair of deuces going nowhere.

They found a bar and drank beer through the afternoon, Jack telling Ennis about a lightning storm on the mountain the year before that killed forty-two sheep, the peculiar stink of them and the way they bloated, the need for plenty of whiskey up there. He had shot an eagle, he said, turned his head to show the tail feather in his hatband. At first glance Jack seemed fair enough with his curly hair and quick laugh, but for a small man he carried some weight in the haunch and his smile disclosed buckteeth, not pronounced enough to let him eat popcorn out of the neck of a jug, but noticeable. He was infatuated with the rodeo life and fastened his belt with a minor bull-riding buckle, but his boots were worn to the quick, holed beyond repair and he was crazy to be somewhere, anywhere else than Lightning Flat.

Ennis, high-arched nose and narrow face, was scruffy and a little cave-chested, balanced a small torso on long, caliper legs, possessed a muscular and supple body made for the horse and for fighting. His reflexes were uncommonly quick and he was farsighted enough to dislike reading anything except Hamley's saddle catalog.

1 Look at the first paragraph. List four things about Ennis del Mar. (4 marks)

....

....

....

....

2 Referring to paragraphs two, five, and six, how has the writer used language to describe Jack and Ennis? (8 marks)
(Write your answer on a separate piece of paper.)

3 You now need to think about the whole of the extract. This text is from the opening pages of a short story. How has the writer structured the text to interest you as a reader?
You could write about:
➤ what the writer focused your attention on at the beginning
➤ how and why the writer alters this focus as the extract develops
➤ any other structural features that interest you. (8 marks)
(Write your answer on a separate piece of paper.)

4 A student, having read paragraphs three and four of the extract said: 'The writer quickly builds up a strong impression of the boss, Joe Aguirre.' To what extent do you agree?
In your response, you should:
➤ write about your own impression of Joe Aguirre
➤ evaluate how the writer has created these impressions
➤ support your opinions with quotations from the text. (20 marks)
(Write your answer on a separate piece of paper.)

5 Compare how Annie Proulx and the author of your set modern text introduce their main characters. Focus on the first two paragraphs of the extract and choose a section from your modern text that introduces one or more of the main characters.
You might consider:
➤ the characters' backgrounds
➤ what they look like and how they behave. (20 marks)
(Write your answer on a separate piece of paper.)

6 Compare how Annie Proulx and the author of your set modern text use dialogue. Focus on the fourth paragraph of the extract and choose one interesting section of dialogue from your modern text.
You might consider:
➤ different ways the dialogue shows things about the speaker
➤ how the dialogue shows things about the setting. (20 marks)
(Write your answer on a separate piece of paper.)

For more help on this topic, see Letts GCSE English Revision Guide pages 16–24.

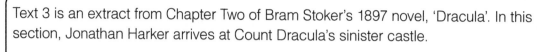
Text 3 is an extract from Chapter Two of Bram Stoker's 1897 novel, 'Dracula'. In this section, Jonathan Harker arrives at Count Dracula's sinister castle.

Text 3

JONATHAN HARKER'S JOURNAL (continued)

5 May. I must have been asleep, for certainly if I had been fully awake I must have noticed the approach of such a remarkable place. In the gloom the courtyard looked of considerable size, and as several dark ways led from it under great round arches, it perhaps seemed bigger than it really is. I have not yet been able to see it by daylight.

When the calèche stopped, the driver jumped down and held out his hand to assist me to alight. Again I could not but notice his prodigious strength. His hand actually seemed like a steel vice that could have crushed mine if he had chosen. Then he took out my traps, and placed them on the ground beside me as I stood close to a great door, old and studded with large iron nails, and set in a projecting doorway of massive stone. I could see even in the dim light that the stone was massively carved, but that the carving had been much worn by time and weather. As I stood, the driver jumped again into his seat and shook the reins; the horses started forward, and trap and all disappeared down one of the dark openings.

I stood in silence where I was, for I did not know what to do. Of bell or knocker there was no sign; through these frowning walls and dark window openings it was not likely that my voice could penetrate. The time I waited seemed endless, and I felt doubts and fears crowding upon me. What sort of place had I come to, and among what kind of people? What sort of grim adventure was it on which I had embarked? Was this a customary incident in the life of a solicitor's clerk sent out to explain the purchase of a London estate to a foreigner? Solicitor's clerk! Mina would not like that. Solicitor – for just before leaving London I got word that my examination was successful; and I am now a full-blown solicitor! I began to rub my eyes and pinch myself to see if I were awake. It all seemed like a horrible nightmare to me, and I expected that I should suddenly awake, and find myself at home, with the dawn struggling in through the windows, as I had now and again felt in the morning after a day of overwork. But my flesh answered the pinching test, and my eyes were not to be deceived. I was indeed awake and among the Carpathians. All I could do now was to be patient, and to wait the coming of the morning.

Just as I had come to this conclusion I heard a heavy step approaching behind the great door, and saw through the chinks the gleam of a coming light. Then there was the sound of rattling chains and the clanking of massive bolts drawn back. A key was turned with the loud grating noise of long disuse, and the great door swung back.

1 From the first paragraph, identify a phrase that shows Harker arrives at the castle after dark.

(1 mark)

....

....

2 From the first paragraph, identify a phrase that suggests Harker's journey has been tiring.

(1 mark)

....

....

3 From the first paragraph, give two ways that Harker appears impressed by the appearance of the castle. Use your own words or quotations from the text. (2 marks)

....

....

....

4 From the second paragraph, give two ways the driver's behaviour seems impolite or strange. Use your own words or quotations from the text. (2 marks)

....

....

....

5 In the second paragraph, how does the writer use language to make the castle sound large and old? Support your views with detailed reference to the text. (4 marks)

....

....

....

....

....

6 In the first five lines of the third paragraph, how does the writer use language to show Harker's thoughts and feelings? Support your views with detailed reference to the text. (4 marks)

....

....

....

....

....

7 In this extract, the writer attempts to engage the reader by building up an eerie atmosphere. Evaluate how effectively the writer does this. Support your views with detailed reference to the text. (8 marks)
(Write your answer on a separate piece of paper.)

8 In this extract, the writer attempts to engage the reader by establishing an unusual setting. Evaluate how effectively the writer does this. Support your views with detailed reference to the text. (8 marks)
(Write your answer on a separate piece of paper.)

For more help on this topic, see Letts GCSE English Revision Guide pages 16–24.

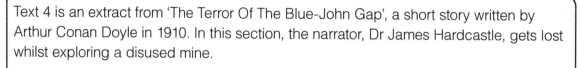

Text 4 is an extract from 'The Terror Of The Blue-John Gap', a short story written by Arthur Conan Doyle in 1910. In this section, the narrator, Dr James Hardcastle, gets lost whilst exploring a disused mine.

Text 4

And now I come to the point where I met with such sudden and desperate disaster. A stream, some twenty feet broad, ran across my path, and I walked for some little distance along the bank to find a spot where I could cross dry-shod. Finally, I came to a place where a single flat boulder lay near the centre, which I could reach in a stride. As it chanced, however, the rock had been cut away and made top-heavy by the rush of the stream, so that it tilted over as I landed on it and shot me into the ice-cold water. My candle went out, and I found myself floundering about in utter and absolute darkness.

I staggered to my feet again, more amused than alarmed by my adventure. The candle had fallen from my hand, and was lost in the stream, but I had two others in my pocket, so that it was of no importance. I got one of them ready, and drew out my box of matches to light it. Only then did I realize my position. The box had been soaked in my fall into the river. It was impossible to strike the matches.

A cold hand seemed to close round my heart as I realized my position. The darkness was opaque and horrible. It was so utter, one put one's hand up to one's face as if to press off something solid. I stood still, and by an effort I steadied myself. I tried to reconstruct in my mind a map of the floor of the cavern as I had last seen it. Alas! the bearings which had impressed themselves upon my mind were high on the wall, and not to be found by touch. Still, I remembered in a general way how the sides were situated, and I hoped that by groping my way along them I should at last come to the opening of the Roman tunnel. Moving very slowly, and continually striking against the rocks, I set out on this desperate quest.

But I very soon realized how impossible it was. In that black, velvety darkness one lost all one's bearings in an instant. Before I had made a dozen paces, I was utterly bewildered as to my whereabouts. The rippling of the stream, which was the one sound audible, showed me where it lay, but the moment that I left its bank I was utterly lost. The idea of finding my way back in absolute darkness through that limestone labyrinth was clearly an impossible one.

I sat down upon a boulder and reflected upon my unfortunate plight. I had not told anyone that I proposed to come to the Blue John mine, and it was unlikely that a search party would come after me. Therefore I must trust to my own resources to get clear of the danger. There was only one hope, and that was that the matches might dry. When I fell into the river, only half of me had got thoroughly wet. My left shoulder had remained above the water. I took the box of matches, therefore, and put it into my left armpit. The moist air of the cavern might possibly be counteracted by the heat of my body, but even so, I knew that I could not hope to get a light for many hours. Meanwhile there was nothing for it but to wait. Gradually, lulled by the monotonous gurgle of the stream, and by the absolute darkness, I sank into an uneasy slumber.

How long this lasted I cannot say. It may have been for an hour, it may have been for several. Suddenly I sat up on my rock couch, with every nerve thrilling and every sense acutely on the alert. Beyond all doubt I had heard a sound - some sound very distinct

Unseen Fiction

from the gurgling of the waters. It had passed, but the reverberation of it still lingered in my ear. Was it a search party? They would most certainly have shouted, and vague as this sound was which had wakened me, it was very distinct from the human voice. I sat palpitating and hardly daring to breathe. There it was again! And again! Now it had become continuous. It was a tread - yes, surely it was the tread of some living creature. But what a tread it was! It gave one the impression of enormous weight carried upon sponge-like feet, which gave forth a muffled but ear-filling sound. The darkness was as complete as ever, but the tread was regular and decisive. And it was coming beyond all question in my direction.

1 From the first paragraph, identify a phrase that suggests something bad is going to happen. (1 mark)

....

2 From the first paragraph, identify a phrase that explains why the rock 'tilted over'. (1 mark)

....

3 From the second paragraph, give two ways that Hardcastle does not seem bothered by what has happened. Use your own words or quotations from the text. (2 marks)

....

....

4 From the fifth paragraph, give two reasons why Hardcastle thinks he is unlikely to get any help in escaping the mine. Use your own words or quotations from the text. (2 marks)

....

....

5 In the third paragraph, how does the writer use language to show Hardcastle's different thoughts and feelings? Support your views with detailed reference to the text. (4 marks)
(Write your answer on a separate piece of paper.)

6 In the fourth paragraph, how does the writer use language to create an atmosphere of hopelessness? Support your views with detailed reference to the text. (4 marks)
(Write your answer on a separate piece of paper.)

7 In this extract, the writer attempts to engage the reader by establishing a creepy setting. Evaluate how effectively the writer does this. Support your views with detailed reference to the text. (8 marks)
(Write your answer on a separate piece of paper.)

8 In this extract, the writer attempts to engage the reader by building up a threatening atmosphere. Evaluate how effectively the writer does this. Support your views with detailed reference to the text. (8 marks)
(Write your answer on a separate piece of paper.)

For more help on this topic, see Letts GCSE English Revision Guide pages 16–24.

Writing to Inform

(Write your answers to these questions on a separate piece of paper.)

1 Imagine that a celebrity has visited your school. Write an article for the local newspaper that informs readers about the reasons for the visit and what happened during the day. You are not required to include any visual or presentational features.

In your article you should:
➤ explain who the celebrity was and why they were visiting
➤ give details of the different things that took place during the visit
➤ include comments from staff, students, and the celebrity.

(24 marks for content and organisation / 16 marks for technical accuracy)

2 Write an article for the school magazine's regular 'Things I Do' page, telling other students about one of your interests or hobbies. You are not required to include any visual or presentational features.

In your article you should:
➤ introduce what your interest or hobby is
➤ give details about your subject (such as how long you've been doing it, what's involved, etc.)
➤ explain how others can get involved.

(24 marks for content and organisation / 16 marks for technical accuracy)

3 As a freelance writer, you have been employed to write a section about where you live for a guidebook called 'Britain's Towns & Cities'. You are not required to include any visual or presentational features.

In your section you should:
➤ introduce where you live and give some key facts
➤ guide readers about what they could do or visit in your area
➤ give an objective view about your area.

(24 marks for content and organisation / 16 marks for technical accuracy)

4 You have been asked by the Headteacher to write the text for a leaflet to be given to new students in order to tell them all about the school. You are not required to include any visual or presentational features.

In your leaflet you should:
➤ introduce the school and give some key facts
➤ include the kind of information that would help students who are new to the school
➤ give an objective view of the school.

(24 marks for content and organisation / 16 marks for technical accuracy)

5 Think of a real or imaginary local news event. Write an article for the local newspaper that reports what happened. You are not required to include any visual or presentational features.

In your article you should:

➤ explain who, what, where, when and why

➤ develop the report in detail so the readers are fully informed

➤ include comments from eye-witnesses or people involved in the news event.

(24 marks for content and organisation / 16 marks for technical accuracy)

6 Write the text for a presentation to the class about a previous holiday. Tell the class about where you went, where you stayed, and what you got up to. You are not required to include any visual or presentational features.

In your presentation you should:

➤ introduce where you went on holiday, when, and with whom

➤ give information about where you stayed and the different things that you did

➤ present an objective view of the holiday.

(24 marks for content and organisation / 16 marks for technical accuracy)

7 Write the text for a presentation to the class about a specific band, singer, author or television programme that you are interested in. The point of your presentation is to tell people all about your subject. You are not required to include any visual or presentational features.

In your presentation you should:

➤ introduce the subject of your talk with some key facts

➤ give details about your subject (such as hit albums, awards, main actors/characters, etc.)

➤ say what the audience can expect from your subject in the coming months.

(24 marks for content and organisation / 16 marks for technical accuracy)

8 Write a speech for your school assembly, telling other students about a charity that you are interested in. You are not required to include any visual or presentational features.

In your article you should:

➤ introduce what the charity is and give some key facts

➤ give details about the charity (such as the work it does, how it raises money, etc.)

➤ explain how others can get involved.

(24 marks for content and organisation / 16 marks for technical accuracy)

For more help on this topic, see Letts GCSE English Revision Guide pages 26–27.

Writing to Explain

(Write your answers to these questions on a separate piece of paper.)

1 Write a speech for your class about someone you respect. This could be a public figure or someone you know.

In your speech you should:
➤ introduce the person and the things that they have done in their life
➤ explain why you respect them
➤ give examples of their best qualities.

(24 marks for content and organisation / 16 marks for technical accuracy)

2 Write the text for a presentation about the things in the world that make you happy or sad. You are not required to include any visual or presentational features.

In your presentation you should:
➤ introduce the things that make you happy or sad
➤ explain why they make you happy or sad
➤ give examples of these things.

(24 marks for content and organisation / 16 marks for technical accuracy)

3 Write an article for the school magazine about the importance of friends. You are not required to include any visual or presentational features.

In your article you should:
➤ introduce the topic of friends
➤ explain the different reasons why friends are important
➤ give examples of the times when friends can help you.

(24 marks for content and organisation / 16 marks for technical accuracy)

4 Write the text for a school blog about your favourite subject.

In your blog you should:
➤ introduce your favourite subject
➤ explain the different reasons why you like the subject so much
➤ give examples of some of the things that you've enjoyed in the subject over the years.

(24 marks for content and organisation / 16 marks for technical accuracy)

5 Write the text for a presentation to the class about the things in your life that have made you into the person you are. You are not required to include any visual or presentational features.

In your presentation you should:
➤ introduce yourself with some interesting facts
➤ explain the different things that are important in your life
➤ give examples of the things that have shaped your life.

(24 marks for content and organisation / 16 marks for technical accuracy)

6 Write the text for a presentation to the class about which celebrities you'd invite to a party. You are not required to include any visual or presentational features.

In your presentation you should:
➤ introduce the theme of your presentation
➤ give details of the celebrities you would invite
➤ explain the different reasons why you would invite your chosen celebrities.

(24 marks for content and organisation / 16 marks for technical accuracy)

7 Write an open letter to be printed in the local newspaper about what it's like be a teenager.

In your letter you should:
➤ introduce the theme of your letter
➤ explain the good and bad things about being a teenager
➤ give examples of ways in which teenagers are misunderstood by adults.

(24 marks for content and organisation / 16 marks for technical accuracy)

8 Write the text for a presentation to your class about your hopes for the future. You can write about your life or you can think on a larger scale about the world. You are not required to include any visual or presentational features.

In your presentation you should:
➤ introduce the topic of hopes for the future
➤ explain your hopes for the next few years
➤ explain your hopes for the long-term future.

(24 marks for content and organisation / 16 marks for technical accuracy)

For more help on this topic, see Letts GCSE English Revision Guide pages 28–29.

Writing

Writing to Describe

(Write your answers to these questions on a separate piece of paper.)

1 Write a description using contrasts and the theme 'City and Countryside'.

(24 marks for content and organisation / 16 marks for technical accuracy)

2 Write the opening part of a story that is set on an alien planet.

(24 marks for content and organisation / 16 marks for technical accuracy)

3 Write a personal anecdote about an exciting day out.

(24 marks for content and organisation / 16 marks for technical accuracy)

4 Write a description using contrasts and the theme 'Day and Night'.

(24 marks for content and organisation / 16 marks for technical accuracy)

5 Write a description inspired by this image of a strange landscape.

(24 marks for content and organisation / 16 marks for technical accuracy)

6 Imagine your dream house. Write a description that takes your reader on a tour of the property.

(24 marks for content and organisation / 16 marks for technical accuracy)

7 Write a description that uses the theme of 'Extreme Weather'.

(24 marks for content and organisation / 16 marks for technical accuracy)

8 Write the opening part of a story that takes place on a desert island.

(24 marks for content and organisation / 16 marks for technical accuracy)

9 Write the opening part of a story that uses the genre of detective fiction.

(24 marks for content and organisation / 16 marks for technical accuracy)

10 Write a description inspired by this image from a storm.

(24 marks for content and organisation / 16 marks for technical accuracy)

For more help on this topic, see Letts GCSE English Revision Guide pages 30–31.

Writing to Persuade

(Write your answers to these questions on a separate piece of paper.)

1 Write the text for a leaflet, to be given out locally, that persuades people to recycle more. You are not required to include any visual or presentational features.

In your leaflet you should:
➤ introduce the topic of recycling
➤ give ways in which people can increase their recycling
➤ give reasons why people should recycle.

(24 marks for content and organisation / 16 marks for technical accuracy)

2 Write an article for the school magazine in which you encourage students in the lower years to read more regularly. You are not required to include any visual or presentational features.

In your article you should:
➤ get the students' attention about reading
➤ give reasons why students should read more
➤ give examples of good books that they could read.

(24 marks for content and organisation / 16 marks for technical accuracy)

3 Write the text for a presentation that encourages your classmates to watch your favourite television programme or film. You are not required to include any visual or presentational features.

In your presentation you should:
➤ introduce your chosen film or programme
➤ give reasons why you like it
➤ give reasons why your classmates will like it.

(24 marks for content and organisation / 16 marks for technical accuracy)

4 The local council have asked for candidates from your school to become the local 'student spokesperson'. Write a letter of application, persuading them to give you the position.

In your letter you should:
➤ introduce yourself
➤ give reasons why you would be good for the position
➤ give examples of things that you have done that would strengthen your application.

(24 marks for content and organisation / 16 marks for technical accuracy)

5 Write a speech to be given to newcomers to the school, encouraging them to take up a musical instrument or a sport as an after-school activity.

In your speech you should:
➤ introduce the benefits of after-school activities
➤ give reasons why it would be good to learn an instrument or practise a sport
➤ give examples of the different options and why they are good.

(24 marks for content and organisation / 16 marks for technical accuracy)

6 You have been invited to write an article for the travel section of a national newspaper, persuading other people to visit your favourite holiday destination. You are not required to include any visual or presentational features.

In your article you should:
➤ introduce your chosen holiday destination
➤ give reasons why it's such a good place to visit
➤ give examples of the different things that can be enjoyed.

(24 marks for content and organisation / 16 marks for technical accuracy)

7 Write a letter to the local council asking for permission to close the roads around your school in order to organise a big charity street party.

In your letter you should:
➤ introduce your proposal
➤ give reasons why the charity deserves everyone's support
➤ porcuade the council that the party and the road closures won't cause problems.

(24 marks for content and organisation / 16 marks for technical accuracy)

8 Write the text for a leaflet, to be given out at school, that persuades young people to exercise more regularly. You are not required to include any visual or presentational features.

In your leaflet you should:
➤ introduce the topic of exercise
➤ present reasons why exercise is worthwhile
➤ give examples of easy, enjoyable exercises that students could take part in.

(24 marks for content and organisation / 16 marks for technical accuracy)

For more help on this topic, see Letts GCSE English Revision Guide pages 32–33.

Writing to Argue

(Write your answers to these questions on a separate piece of paper.)

1 Write a speech for school assembly, arguing the pros and cons of school uniform.

In your speech you should:
➤ give the argument for school uniform
➤ give the argument against school uniform
➤ conclude with your own judgement.

(24 marks for content and organisation / 16 marks for technical accuracy)

2 Write a speech for school assembly, presenting the arguments for and against banning mobile phones in schools.

In your speech you should:
➤ present the argument for keeping mobile phones
➤ present the argument for banning mobile phones
➤ conclude with your own judgement.

(24 marks for content and organisation / 16 marks for technical accuracy)

3 As part of a school project, you have been asked to present an argument to local councillors about the proposals to build a theme park in your town. Write the text for a presentation about the theme park's pros and cons. You are not required to include any visual or presentational features.

In your presentation you should:
➤ give the argument for the theme park
➤ give the argument against the theme park
➤ conclude with your own judgement about the proposal.

(24 marks for content and organisation / 16 marks for technical accuracy)

4 Write an article for your local newspaper, presenting the different aspects of a recent proposal to change the speed limit for all roads in the county to 40 mph. You are not required to include any visual or presentational features.

In your article you should:
➤ present the pros of altering the speed limit
➤ present the cons of altering the speed limit
➤ conclude with your own judgement about the proposal.

(24 marks for content and organisation / 16 marks for technical accuracy)

5 Write a speech for school assembly, giving the argument for and against decreasing the amount of reality television.

In your speech you should:
➤ give the argument for reality television
➤ give the argument against reality television
➤ conclude with your own judgement.

(24 marks for content and organisation / 16 marks for technical accuracy)

6 Write the text for a presentation to your class about the idea of banning fast food. You are not required to include any visual or presentational features.

In your presentation you should:
➤ present the argument for banning fast food
➤ present the argument against banning fast food
➤ conclude with your own judgement about the issue.

(24 marks for content and organisation / 16 marks for technical accuracy)

7 Write an article for the school magazine in which you present the argument for and against lowering the voting age from 18 to 16. You are not required to include any visual or presentational features.

In your article you should:
➤ give the argument for lowering the voting age to 16
➤ give the argument for keeping the voting age at 18
➤ conclude with your own judgements about the voting age.

(24 marks for content and organisation / 16 marks for technical accuracy)

8 Write an open letter to the local newspaper that presents the different arguments for and against a recent council proposal to establish a 9pm weekday curfew for all young people under the age of 17.

In your letter you should:
➤ present the pros of the curfew
➤ present the cons of the curfew
➤ conclude with your own judgement about the curfew.

(24 marks for content and organisation / 16 marks for technical accuracy)

For more help on this topic, see Letts GCSE English Revision Guide pages 34–35.

Writing

Writing to Advise and Instruct

(Write your answers to these questions on a separate piece of paper.)

1 Write the text for a leaflet to be given out to newcomers to the school, giving them advice about how to settle in. You are not required to include any visual or presentational features.

In your leaflet you should:
➤ welcome new students to the school
➤ identify different issues or problems that students can face when they join a new school
➤ present ideas on how to resolve each of those problems.

(24 marks for content and organisation / 16 marks for technical accuracy)

2 Write the text for a blog about the best ways to revise for exams.

In your blog you should:
➤ introduce the topic of revision
➤ identify different revision methods that can be useful
➤ suggest ways in which young people can cope with the stress of revision.

(24 marks for content and organisation / 16 marks for technical accuracy)

3 Write an article for the advice pages of the school magazine in which you look at friendship issues. You are not required to include any visual or presentational features.

In your article you should:
➤ introduce the theme of friendship issues
➤ identify the different friendship issues that can arise for teenagers
➤ present ways in which these issues can be avoided or resolved.

(24 marks for content and organisation / 16 marks for technical accuracy)

4 Write a speech for school assembly advising people about how to live a healthier lifestyle.

In your speech you should:
➤ get people thinking about the benefits of a healthy lifestyle
➤ identify the different things people can do to achieve a healthier lifestyle
➤ identify the obstacles that people face and how these can be overcome.

(24 marks for content and organisation / 16 marks for technical accuracy)

5 Write an article for the school magazine's advice pages about peer pressure. You are not required to include any visual or presentational features.

In your article you should:
➤ acknowledge the powers of peer pressure
➤ give advice on how to avoid peer pressure
➤ present ways in which you can deal with peer pressure.

(24 marks for content and organisation / 16 marks for technical accuracy)

6 Write the text for a leaflet advising younger students about how to stay safe on fireworks night. You are not required to include any visual or presentational features.

In your leaflet you should:
➤ introduce the theme of fireworks night
➤ give examples of the different dangers that young people need to be aware of
➤ give advice on how to avoid being a victim of any of these dangers.

(24 marks for content and organisation / 16 marks for technical accuracy)

7 Write a speech for school assembly that gives advice about dealing with bullying.

In your speech you should:
➤ introduce the theme of bullying
➤ suggest different strategies for avoiding, or dealing with, bullying
➤ give examples of people in school that can help if you are being bullied.

(24 marks for content and organisation / 16 marks for technical accuracy)

8 Write the text for a leaflet, to be made available to parents, that offers advice on keeping their children healthy on hot summer days. You are not required to include any visual or presentational features.

In your leaflet you should:
➤ introduce the topic of staying healthy in the sun
➤ identify some of the dangers of hot summer weather
➤ give ways in which parents can avoid or reduce these dangers.

(24 marks for content and organisation / 16 marks for technical accuracy)

For more help on this topic, see Letts GCSE English Revision Guide pages 36–37.

Revising Cluster Poetry: Starter Questions

1 What is a simile? Choose an example from any poem in the anthology and explain what idea it conveys. (3 marks)

....

....

2 What is a metaphor? Choose an example from any poem in the anthology and explain what idea it conveys. (3 marks)

....

....

....

3 What is personification? Choose an example from any poem in the anthology and explain what idea it conveys. (3 marks)

....

....

....

4 What are alliteration, onomatopoeia and rhyme? Choose an example of each from any poems in the anthology. Explain the effect each technique has on the poem you chose it from. (9 marks)

....

....

....

....

....

....

....

5 Find an example of each of the following structural devices from anywhere in the anthology: repetition, short sentence, list. Explain how your examples are being used to convey meaning in the poems you chose them from. (6 marks)

....

....

....

....

(Write your answers to these questions on a separate piece of paper.)

Love and Relationships

1 How does one of the poems from the anthology present family relations?
In your answer, you should consider the poet's use of language, structure and form. (15 marks)

2 How does one of the poems from the anthology present love?
In your answer, you should consider the poet's use of language, structure and form. (15 marks)

3 How does one of the poems from the anthology present an unhappy relationship?
In your answer, you should consider the poet's use of language, structure and form. (15 marks)

Conflict and Power

1 How does one of the poems from the anthology present war?
In your answer, you should consider the poet's use of language, structure and form. (15 marks)

2 How does one of the poems from the anthology present feelings?
In your answer, you should consider the poet's use of language, structure and form. (15 marks)

3 How does one of the poems from the anthology present bravery and/or cowardice?
In your answer, you should consider the poet's use of language, structure and form. (15 marks)

Youth and Age

1 How does one of the poems from the anthology present children?
In your answer, you should consider the poet's use of language, structure and form. (15 marks)

2 How does one of the poems in the anthology present death?
In your answer, you should consider the poet's use of language, structure and form. (15 marks)

3 How does one of the poems in the anthology present powerful emotions?
In your answer, you should consider the poet's use of language, structure and form. (15 marks)

Time and Place

1 How does one of the poems in the anthology present the importance of place?
In your answer, you should consider the poet's use of language, structure and form. (15 marks)

2 How does one of the poems in the anthology present a place in a negative way?
In your answer, you should consider the poet's use of language, structure and form. (15 marks)

3 How does one of the poems in the anthology present the beauty of a place?
In your answer, you should consider the poet's use of language, structure and form. (15 marks)

For more help on this topic, see Letts GCSE English Revision Guide pages 46–47.

Analysing Unseen Modern Poetry

1 How does the poet convey the speaker's feelings about the death of a lover?
*(Annotate the poem to get you thinking and then write your answer on a
separate piece of paper.)*

(15 marks)

Funeral Blues
by *W.H. Auden*

Stop all the clocks, cut off the telephone,

Prevent the dog from barking with a juicy bone,

Silence the pianos and with muffled drum

Bring out the coffin, let the mourners come.

Let aeroplanes circle moaning overhead

Scribbling on the sky the message He Is Dead,

Put crepe bows round the white necks of the public doves,

Let the traffic policemen wear black cotton gloves.

He was my North, my South, my East and West,

My working week and my Sunday rest,

My noon, my midnight, my talk, my song;

I thought that love would last for ever: I was wrong.

The stars are not wanted now: put out every one;

Pack up the moon and dismantle the sun;

Pour away the ocean and sweep up the wood.

For nothing now can ever come to any good.

2 How does the poet present his experiences of World War One? (15 marks)

(Annotate the poem to get you thinking and then write your answer on a separate piece of paper.)

Returning We Hear The Larks
by *Isaac Rosenberg*

Sombre the night is.

And though we have our lives, we know

What sinister threat lurks there.

Dragging these anguished limbs, we only know

This poison-blasted track opens on our camp –

On a little safe sleep.

But hark! joy – joy – strange joy.

Lo! heights of night ringing with unseen larks.

Music showering our upturned list'ning faces.

Death could drop from the dark

As easily as song –

But song only dropped,

Like a blind man's dreams on the sand

By dangerous tides,

Like a girl's dark hair for she dreams no ruin lies there,

Or her kisses where a serpent hides.

For more help on this topic, see Letts GCSE English Revision Guide pages 48–49.

Poetry

3 How does the poet present different childhood experiences? (15 marks)
(Write your answer on a separate piece of paper.)

In Mrs Tilscher's Class
by *Carol Ann Duffy*

You could travel up the Blue Nile

with your finger, tracing the route

while Mrs Tilscher chanted the scenery.

'Tana. Ethiopia. Khartoum. Aswan.'

That for an hour,

then a skittle of milk

and the chalky Pyramids rubbed into dust.

A window opened with a long pole.

The laugh of a bell swung by a running child.

This was better than home. Enthralling books.

The classroom glowed like a sweetshop.

Sugar paper. Coloured shapes. Brady and Hindley

faded, like the faint, uneasy smudge of a mistake.

Mrs Tilscher loved you. Some mornings, you found

she'd left a gold star by your name.

The scent of a pencil slowly, carefully, shaved.

A xylophone's nonsense heard from another form.

Over the Easter term the inky tadpoles changed

from commas into exclamation marks. Three frogs

hopped in the playground, freed by a dunce

followed by a line of kids, jumping and croaking

away from the lunch queue. A rough boy

told you how you were born. You kicked him, but stared

at your parents, appalled, when you got back home.

That feverish July, the air tasted of electricity.

A tangible alarm made you always untidy, hot,

fractious under the heavy, sexy sky. You asked her

how you were born and Mrs Tilscher smiled

then turned away. Reports were handed out.

You ran through the gates, impatient to be grown

the sky split open into a thunderstorm.

4 How does the poet present ideas about nature? (15 marks)
(Write your answer on a separate piece of paper.)

Trees
by *Philip Larkin*

The trees are coming into leaf
Like something almost being said;
The recent buds relax and spread,
Their greenness is a kind of grief.

Is it that they are born again
And we grow old? No, they die too,
Their yearly trick of looking new
Is written down in rings of grain.

Yet still the unresting castles thresh
In full-grown thickness every May.
Last year is dead, they seem to say,
Begin afresh, afresh, afresh.

For more help on this topic, see Letts GCSE English Revision Guide pages 48–49.

Analysing Unseen Heritage Poetry

1 How does the poet present the shepherd's feelings for the woman he loves?
(Write your answer on a separate piece of paper.) (15 marks)

The Passionate Shepherd To His Love
by *Christopher Marlowe*

Come live with me and be my Love,
And we will all the pleasures prove
That hills and valleys, dale and field,
And all the craggy mountains yield.

There will we sit upon the rocks
And see the shepherds feed their flocks,
By shallow rivers, to whose falls
Melodious birds sing madrigals.

There will I make thee beds of roses
And a thousand fragrant posies,
A cap of flowers, and a kirtle
Embroider'd all with leaves of myrtle.

A gown made of the finest wool
Which from our pretty lambs we pull,
Fair linèd slippers for the cold,
With buckles of the purest gold.

A belt of straw and ivy buds
With coral clasps and amber studs:
And if these pleasures may thee move,
Come live with me and be my Love.

Thy silver dishes for thy meat
As precious as the gods do eat,
Shall on an ivory table be
Prepared each day for thee and me.

The shepherd swains shall dance and sing
For thy delight each May-morning:
If these delights thy mind may move,
Then live with me and be my Love.

2 How does the poet present his ideas about the death of an unknown soldier?   (15 marks)
(Write your answer on a separate piece of paper.)

Dirge For A Soldier
G.H. Boker

Close his eyes; his work is done!
What to him is friend or foeman,
Rise of moon, or set of sun,
Hand of man, or kiss of woman?

Lay him low, lay him low,
In the clover or the snow!
What cares he? He cannot know;
Lay him low!

As man may, he fought his fight,
Proved his truth by his endeavour;
Let him sleep in solemn night,
Sleep for ever and for ever.

Fold him in his country's stars,
Roll the drum and fire the volley!
What to him are all our wars,
What but death bemocking folly?

Leave him to God's watching eye;
Trust him to the hand that made him.
Mortal love weeps idly by;
God alone has power to aid him.

Lay him low, lay him low,
In the clover or the snow!
What cares he? He cannot know!
Lay him low!

For more help on this topic, see Letts GCSE English Revision Guide pages 50–51.

3 How does the poet present the experience of children who were forced to be chimney sweepers in the 19th century? (15 marks)

(Write your answer on a separate piece of paper.)

The Chimney Sweeper
by *William Blake*

When my mother died I was very young,
And my father sold me while yet my tongue
Could scarcely cry 'weep weep weep weep!'
So your chimneys I sweep, and in soot I sleep.

There's little Tom Dacre, who cried when his head
That curled like a lamb's back, was shaved, so I said,
'Hush, Tom! Never mind it, for when your head's bare,
You know that the soot cannot spoil your white hair.'

And so he was quiet, and that very night,
As Tom was a-sleeping he had such a sight!
That thousands of sweepers, Dick, Joe, Ned, and Jack,
Were all of them locked up in coffins of black.

And by came an angel who had a bright key,
And he opened the coffins and set them all free;
Then down a green plain leaping, laughing they run
And wash in a river, and shine in the sun.

Then naked and white, all their bags left behind,
They rise upon clouds, and sport in the wind.
And the angel told Tom, if he'd be a good boy,
He'd have God for his father and never want joy.

And so Tom awoke, and we rose in the dark,
And got with our bags and our brushes to work;
Though the morning was cold, Tom was happy & warm –
So if all do their duty, they need not fear harm.

4 How does the poet present his feelings about nature? (15 marks)
(Write your answer on a separate piece of paper.)

Daffodils
by *William Wordsworth*

I wander'd lonely as a cloud
That floats on high o'er vales and hills,
When all at once I saw a crowd,
A host of golden daffodils,
Beside the lake, beneath the trees
Fluttering and dancing in the breeze.

Continuous as the stars that shine
And twinkle on the milky way,
They stretch'd in never-ending line
Along the margin of a bay:
Ten thousand saw I at a glance
Tossing their heads in sprightly dance.

The waves beside them danced, but they
Out-did the sparkling waves in glee: -
A poet could not but be gay
In such a jocund company!
I gazed - and gazed - but little thought
What wealth the show to me had brought.

For oft, when on my couch I lie
In vacant or in pensive mood,
They flash upon that inward eye
Which is the bliss of solitude;
And then my heart with pleasure fills
And dances with the daffodils.

For more help on this topic, see Letts GCSE English Revision Guide pages 50–51.

Comparing Modern Unseen Poetry / Comparing Modern and Heritage Unseen Poetry
(Write your answers on a separate piece of paper.)

1 Compare the ways the poets present love in W.H. Auden's 'Funeral Blues' (page 34) and Christopher Marlowe's 'The Passionate Shepherd To His Love' (page 38).

Compare:
➤ the ideas in the poems
➤ the poets' use of language
➤ the poets' use of form and structure. (30 marks)

2 Compare the presentation of loss in W.H. Auden's 'Funeral Blues' (page 34) and a poem from the anthology.

Compare:
➤ the ideas in the poems
➤ the poets' use of language
➤ the poets' use of form and structure. (30 marks)

3 Compare how the poets present powerful emotions in two poems from the anthology.

Compare:
➤ the ideas in the poems
➤ the poets' use of language
➤ the poets' use of form and structure. (30 marks)

4 Compare the ways the poets present experiences of war in Isaac Rosenberg's 'Returning We Hear The Larks' (page 35) and G.H. Boker's 'Dirge For A Soldier' (page 39).

Compare:
➤ the ideas in the poems
➤ the poets' use of language
➤ the poets' use of form and structure. (30 marks)

5 Compare the presentation of war in Isaac Rosenberg's 'Returning We Hear The Larks' (page 35) and a poem from the anthology.

Compare:
➤ the ideas in the poems
➤ the poets' use of language
➤ the poets' use of form and structure. (30 marks)

6 Compare how the poets present different attitudes to fighting in two poems from the anthology.

Compare:
➤ the ideas in the poems
➤ the poets' use of language
➤ the poets' use of form and structure. (30 marks)

7 Compare the ways the poets present childhood in Carol Ann Duffy's 'In Mrs Tilscher's Class' (page 36) and William Blake's 'The Chimney Sweeper' (page 40).

Compare:
➤ the ideas in the poems
➤ the poets' use of language
➤ the poets' use of form and structure. (30 marks)

8 Compare the presentation of children in Carol Ann Duffy's 'In Mrs Tilscher's Class' (page 36) and one poem from the anthology.

Compare:
➤ the ideas in the poems
➤ the poets' use of language
➤ the poets' use of form and structure. (30 marks)

9 Compare how the poets present different attitudes to growing up or getting old in two poems from the anthology.

Compare:
➤ the ideas in the poems
➤ the poets' use of language
➤ the poets' use of form and structure. (30 marks)

10 Compare the ways the poets present their responses to nature in Philip Larkin's 'Trees' (page 37) and William Wordsworth's 'Daffodils' (page 41).

Compare:
➤ the ideas in the poems
➤ the poets' use of language
➤ the poets' use of form and structure. (30 marks)

11 Compare the presentation of nature in Philip Larkin's 'Trees' (page 37) and one poem from the anthology.

Compare:
➤ the ideas in the poems
➤ the poets' use of language
➤ the poets' use of form and structure. (30 marks)

12 Compare how the poets present strong feelings about a place in two of the poems from the anthology.

Compare:
➤ the ideas in the poems
➤ the poets' use of language
➤ the poets' use of form and structure. (30 marks)

For more help on this topic, see Letts GCSE English Revision Guide pages 52–55.

ROMEO AND JULIET (ACT 1 SCENE 1)

(Write your answers on a separate piece of paper.)

1 **a)** How does Shakespeare present the relationship between Romeo and Benvolio in this extract? (15 marks)

   b) How does Shakespeare present friendships in the play as a whole? (15 marks)

2 How does Shakespeare present the difficulties of being in love in the play as a whole? (30 marks)

At this point in the play, Romeo is explaining to Benvolio how Rosalind does not love him back.

BENVOLIO	What sadness lengthens Romeo's hours?
ROMEO	Not having that, which, having, makes them short.
BENVOLIO	In love?
ROMEO	Out –
BENVOLIO	Of love?
ROMEO	Out of her favour, where I am in love.
BENVOLIO	Alas, that love, so gentle in his view,
	Should be so tyrannous and rough in proof!
ROMEO	Alas, that love, whose view is muffled still,
	Should, without eyes, see pathways to his will!
	Where shall we dine? O me! What fray was here?
	Yet tell me not, for I have heard it all.
	Here's much to do with hate, but more with love.
	Why, then, O brawling love! O loving hate!
	O any thing, of nothing first create!
	O heavy lightness! serious vanity!
	Mis-shapen chaos of well-seeming forms!
	Feather of lead, bright smoke, cold fire, sick health!
	Still-waking sleep, that is not what it is!
	This love feel I, that feel no love in this.
	Dost thou not laugh?
BENVOLIO	No, coz, I rather weep.
ROMEO	Good heart, at what?
BENVOLIO	At thy good heart's oppression.
ROMEO	Why, such is love's transgression.
	Griefs of mine own lie heavy in my breast,
	Which thou wilt propagate, to have it prest
	With more of thine: this love that thou hast shown
	Doth add more grief to too much of mine own.
	Love is a smoke raised with the fume of sighs;
	Being purged, a fire sparkling in lovers' eyes;
	Being vex'd a sea nourish'd with lovers' tears:
	What is it else? a madness most discreet,
	A choking gall and a preserving sweet.
	Farewell, my coz

ROMEO AND JULIET (ACT 4 SCENE 5)

(Write your answers on a separate piece of paper.)

1 **a)** How does Shakespeare present Lord and Lady Capulet's grief for their daughter in
this extract? (15 marks)
b) How are Lord and Lady Capulet presented in the play as a whole? (15 marks)

2 How does Shakespeare present the Nurse in the play as a whole? (30 marks)

*At this point in the play, on the morning of her wedding to Paris, Juliet has faked her death and is
discovered by the Nurse and her parents.*

LADY CAPULET	What noise is here?
NURSE	O lamentable day!
LADY CAPULET	What is the matter?
NURSE	Look, look! O heavy day!
LADY CAPULET	O me, O me! My child, my only life,
	Revive, look up, or I will die with thee!
	Help, help! Call help.
	*(Enter **Capulet**)*
CAPULET	For shame, bring Juliet forth; her lord is come.
NURSE	She's dead, deceased, she's dead; alack the day!
LADY CAPULET	Alack the day, she's dead, she's dead, she's dead!
CAPULET	Ha! let me see her: out, alas! she's cold:
	Her blood is settled, and her joints are stiff;
	Life and these lips have long been separated:
	Death lies on her like an untimely frost
	Upon the sweetest flower of all the field.
NURSE	O lamentable day!
LADY CAPULET	O woeful time!
CAPULET	Death, that hath ta'en her hence to make me wail,
	Ties up my tongue, and will not let me speak.
	*(Enter **Friar Laurence** and **Paris**, with Musicians)*
FRIAR LAURENCE	Come, is the bride ready to go to church?
CAPULET	Ready to go, but never to return.
	O son! the night before thy wedding-day
	Hath Death lain with thy wife. There she lies,
	Flower as she was, deflowered by him.
	Death is my son-in-law, Death is my heir;
	My daughter he hath wedded: I will die,
	And leave him all; life, living, all is Death's.

For more help on this topic, see Letts GCSE English Revision Guide pages 58–68.

Shakespeare

THE MERCHANT OF VENICE (ACT 1 SCENE 3)

(Write your answers on a separate piece of paper.)

1 a) How does Shakespeare present Shylock's dislike of Antonio in this extract? *(15 marks)*

b) To what extent does Shakespeare present Shylock as a dislikeable character in the play as a whole? *(15 marks)*

2 How does Shakespeare present the theme of greed in the play as a whole? *(30 marks)*

At this point in the play, Shylock is considering Bassanio's request for a loan.

SHYLOCK	Three thousand ducats; I think I may take his bond.
BASSANIO	Be assured you may.
SHYLOCK	I will be assured I may; and, that I may be assured, I will bethink me. May I speak with Antonio?
BASSANIO	If it please you to dine with us.
SHYLOCK	Yes, to smell pork; to eat of the habitation which your prophet the Nazarite conjured the devil into. I will buy with you, sell with you, talk with you, walk with you, and so following, but I will not eat with you, drink with you, nor pray with you. What news on the Rialto? Who is he comes here? *(Enter **Antonio**)*
BASSANIO	This is Signior Antonio.
SHYLOCK (*Aside*)	How like a fawning publican he looks! I hate him for he is a Christian, But more for that in low simplicity He lends out money gratis and brings down The rate of usance here with us in Venice. If I can catch him once upon the hip, I will feed fat the ancient grudge I bear him. He hates our sacred nation, and he rails, Even there where merchants most do congregate, On me, my bargains and my well-won thrift, Which he calls interest. Cursed be my tribe, If I forgive him!
BASSANIO	Shylock, do you hear?
SHYLOCK	I am debating of my present store, And, by the near guess of my memory, I cannot instantly raise up the gross Of full three thousand ducats. What of that? Tubal, a wealthy Hebrew of my tribe, Will furnish me. But soft! how many months Do you desire? (*To **Antonio***) Rest you fair, good signior; Your worship was the last man in our mouths.

THE MERCHANT OF VENICE (ACT 1 SCENE 2)

(Write your answers on a separate piece of paper.)

1 **a)** How does Shakespeare present the relationship between Portia and Nerissa in
this extract? (15 marks)

b) How does Shakespeare present the relationship between Portia and Nerissa in the
play as a whole? (15 marks)

2 How does the character of Portia develop during the play as a whole and how does Shakespeare
show this? (30 marks)

At this point in the play, Portia is discussing her feelings about her current situation with Nerissa.

PORTIA	By my troth, Nerissa, my little body is aweary of this great world.
NERISSA	You would be, sweet madam, if your miseries were in the same abundance as your good fortunes are: and yet, for aught I see, they are as sick that surfeit with too much as they that starve with nothing. It is no mean happiness therefore, to be seated in the mean: superfluity comes sooner by white hairs, but competency lives longer.
PORTIA	Good sentences and well pronounced.
NERISSA	They would be better, if well followed.
PORTIA	If to do were as easy as to know what were good to do, chapels had been churches and poor men's cottages princes' palaces. It is a good divine that follows his own instructions: I can easier teach twenty what were good to be done, than be one of the twenty to follow mine own teaching. The brain may devise laws for the blood, but a hot temper leaps o'er a cold decree: such a hare is madness the youth, to skip o'er the meshes of good counsel the cripple. But this reasoning is not in the fashion to choose me a husband. O me, the word 'choose!' I may neither choose whom I would nor refuse whom I dislike; so is the will of a living daughter curbed by the will of a dead father. Is it not hard, Nerissa, that I cannot choose one nor refuse none?
NERISSA	Your father was ever virtuous; and holy men at their death have good inspirations: therefore the lottery, that he hath devised in these three chests of gold, silver and lead, whereof who chooses his meaning chooses you, will, no doubt, never be chosen by any rightly but one who shall rightly love. But what warmth is there in your affection towards any of these princely suitors that are already come?
PORTIA	I pray thee, over-name them; and as thou namest them, I will describe them; and, according to my description, level at my affection.

For more help on this topic, see Letts GCSE English Revision Guide pages 58–68.

Shakespeare

MACBETH (ACT 3 SCENE 4)

(Write your answers on a separate piece of paper.)

1 **a)** How does Shakespeare present the character of Macbeth in this extract? (15 marks)

b) How does Shakespeare present the different aspects of Macbeth's character in the play as a whole? (15 marks)

2 How does Shakespeare present Macbeth's anxieties in the play as a whole? (30 marks)

At this point in the play, Macbeth is recently crowned king and is holding a banquet. He has sent murderers to kill Banquo and Fleance.

MACBETH	You know your own degrees; sit down: at first And last the hearty welcome.
LORDS	Thanks to your majesty.
MACBETH	Ourself will mingle with society, And play the humble host. Our hostess keeps her state, but in best time We will require her welcome.
LADY MACBETH	Pronounce it for me, sir, to all our friends; For my heart speaks they are welcome. *(First Murderer appears at the door)*
MACBETH	See, they encounter thee with their hearts' thanks. Both sides are even: here I'll sit i' the midst: Be large in mirth; anon we'll drink a measure The table round. *(Approaching the door)* There's blood on thy face.
FIRST MURDERER	'Tis Banquo's then.
MACBETH	'Tis better thee without than he within. Is he dispatch'd?
FIRST MURDERER	My lord, his throat is cut; that I did for him.
MACBETH	Thou art the best o' the cut-throats: yet he's good That did the like for Fleance: if thou didst it, Thou art the nonpareil.
FIRST MURDERER	Most royal sir, Fleance is 'scaped.
MACBETH	Then comes my fit again: I had else been perfect, Whole as the marble, founded as the rock, As broad and general as the casing air: But now I am cabin'd, cribb'd, confined, bound in To saucy doubts and fears. But Banquo's safe?
FIRST MURDERER	Ay, my good lord: safe in a ditch he bides, With twenty trenched gashes on his head; The least a death to nature.

MACBETH (ACT 1 SCENE 7)

(Write your answers on a separate piece of paper.)

1 **a)** How does Shakespeare present the character of Lady Macbeth in this extract? (15 marks)

b) How does Shakespeare present Lady Macbeth in the play as a whole? (15 marks)

2 How does Shakespeare present the theme of manipulation in the play as a whole? (30 marks)

At this point in the play, King Duncan is at Dunsinane Castle. Despite initially agreeing to his wife's plan to kill the king, Macbeth has changed his mind.

MACBETH	We will proceed no further in this business:
	He hath honour'd me of late; and I have bought
	Golden opinions from all sorts of people,
	Which would be worn now in their newest gloss,
	Not cast aside so soon.
LADY MACBETH	Was the hope drunk
	Wherein you dress'd yourself? hath it slept since?
	And wakes it now, to look so green and pale
	At what it did so freely? From this time
	Such I account thy love. Art thou afeard
	To be the same in thine own act and valour
	As thou art in desire? Wouldst thou have that
	Which thou esteem'st the ornament of life,
	And live a coward in thine own esteem,
	Letting 'I dare not' wait upon 'I would,'
	Like the poor cat i' the adage?
MACBETH	Prithee, peace:
	I dare do all that may become a man;
	Who dares do more is none.
LADY MACBETH	What beast was't, then,
	That made you break this enterprise to me?
	When you durst do it, then you were a man;
	And, to be more than what you were, you would
	Be so much more the man. Nor time nor place
	Did then adhere, and yet you would make both:
	They have made themselves, and that their fitness now
	Does unmake you. I have given suck, and know
	How tender 'tis to love the babe that milks me:
	I would, while it was smiling in my face,
	Have pluck'd my nipple from his boneless gums,
	And dash'd the brains out, had I so sworn as you
	Have done to this.
MACBETH	If we should fail?
LADY MACBETH	We fail!
	But screw your courage to the sticking-place,
	And we'll not fail.

For more help on this topic, see Letts GCSE English Revision Guide pages 58–68.

MUCH ADO ABOUT NOTHING (ACT 1 SCENE 1)

(Write your answers on a separate piece of paper.)

1 **a)** How does Shakespeare present the relationship between Beatrice and Benedick in this extract? (15 marks)

b) How does Shakespeare present Beatrice's feelings about Benedick in the play as a whole? (15 marks)

2 How does Shakespeare present Benedick's changing feelings about love and marriage in the play as a whole? (30 marks)

At this point in the play, Don Pedro and his men have arrived at Leonato's house and are being welcomed.

BENEDICK	If Signior Leonato be her father, she would not have his head on her shoulders for all Messina, as like him as she is.
BEATRICE	I wonder that you will still be talking, Signior Benedick: nobody marks you.
BENEDICK	What, my dear Lady Disdain! are you yet living?
BEATRICE	Is it possible disdain should die while she hath such meet food to feed it as Signior Benedick? Courtesy itself must convert to disdain, if you come in her presence.
BENEDICK	Then is courtesy a turncoat. But it is certain I am loved of all ladies, only you excepted: and I would I could find in my heart that I had not a hard heart; for, truly, I love none.
BEATRICE	A dear happiness to women: they would else have been troubled with a pernicious suitor. I thank God and my cold blood, I am of your humour for that: I had rather hear my dog bark at a crow than a man swear he loves me.
BENEDICK	God keep your ladyship still in that mind! so some gentleman or other shall 'scape a predestinate scratched face.
BEATRICE	Scratching could not make it worse, an 'twere such a face as yours were.
BENEDICK	Well, you are a rare parrot-teacher.
BEATRICE	A bird of my tongue is better than a beast of yours.
BENEDICK	I would my horse had the speed of your tongue, and so good a continuer. But keep your way, i' God's name; I have done.
BEATRICE	You always end with a jade's trick: I know you of old.

MUCH ADO ABOUT NOTHING (ACT 3 SCENE 2)

(Write your answers on a separate piece of paper.)

1 **a)** How does Shakespeare present the character of Don John in this extract? (15 marks)

    b) How does Shakespeare present the character of Don John in the play as a whole? (15 marks)

2 How does Shakespeare present the theme of deception in the play as a whole? (30 marks)

At this point in the play, it is the night before Claudio's wedding to Hero; Don John arrives with a plan to ruin the happy day.

DON JOHN	You may think I love you not: let that appear hereafter, and aim better at me by that I now will manifest. For my brother, I think he holds you well, and in dearness of heart hath help to effect your ensuing marriage – surely suit ill spent and labour ill bestowed.
DON PEDRO	Why, what's the matter?
DON JOHN	I came hither to tell you; and, circumstances shortened, for she has been too long a talking of, the lady is disloyal.
CLAUDIO	Who, Hero?
DON PEDRO	Even she; Leonato's Hero, your Hero, every man's Hero:
CLAUDIO	Disloyal?
DON JOHN	The word is too good to paint out her wickedness; I could say she were worse: think you of a worse title, and I will fit her to it. Wonder not till further warrant: go but with me to-night, you shall see her chamber-window entered, even the night before her wedding-day: if you love her then, to-morrow wed her; but it would better fit your honour to change your mind.
CLAUDIO	May this be so?
DON PEDRO	I will not think it.
DON JOHN	If you dare not trust that you see, confess not that you know: if you will follow me, I will show you enough; and when you have seen more and heard more, proceed accordingly.
CLAUDIO	If I see any thing to-night why I should not marry her to-morrow in the congregation, where I should wed, there will I shame her.
DON PEDRO	And, as I wooed for thee to obtain her, I will join with thee to disgrace her.
DON JOHN	I will disparage her no farther till you are my witnesses: bear it coldly but till midnight, and let the issue show itself.
DON PEDRO	O day untowardly turned!
CLAUDIO	O mischief strangely thwarting!
DON JOHN	O plague right well prevented! so will you say when you have seen the sequel.

For more help on this topic, see Letts GCSE English Revision Guide pages 58–68.

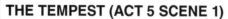

THE TEMPEST (ACT 5 SCENE 1)

(Write your answers on a separate piece of paper.)

1 **a)** In this extract, how does Shakespeare show that Prospero's actions have not been driven by a wish for revenge? (15 marks)

b) How does Shakespeare show Prospero judging and punishing different characters in the play as a whole? (15 marks)

2 How does Shakespeare show different aspects of Prospero's character in the play as a whole? (30 marks)

At this point in the play, Prospero traps Gonzalo, Alonso, Sebastian and Antonio in a magic circle before giving his judgement on each of them.

*(Re-enter **Ariel** before: then **Alonso**, with a frantic gesture, attended by **Gonzalo**; **Sebastian** and **Antonio** in like manner, attended by **Adrian** and **Francisco** they all enter the circle which **Prospero** had made, and there stand charmed; which **PROSPERO** observing, speaks:)*
A solemn air and the best comforter
To an unsettled fancy cure thy brains,
Now useless, boil'd within thy skull! There stand,
For you are spell-stopp'd.
Holy Gonzalo, honourable man,
Mine eyes, even sociable to the show of thine,
Fall fellowly drops. The charm dissolves apace,
And as the morning steals upon the night,
Melting the darkness, so their rising senses
Begin to chase the ignorant fumes that mantle
Their clearer reason. O good Gonzalo,
My true preserver, and a loyal sir
To him you follow'st! I will pay thy graces
Home both in word and deed. Most cruelly
Didst thou, Alonso, use me and my daughter:
Thy brother was a furtherer in the act.
Thou art pinch'd fort now, Sebastian. Flesh and blood,
You, brother mine, that entertain'd ambition,
Expell'd remorse and nature; who, with Sebastian,
Whose inward pinches therefore are most strong,
Would here have kill'd your king; I do forgive thee,
Unnatural though thou art. Their understanding
Begins to swell, and the approaching tide
Will shortly fill the reasonable shore
That now lies foul and muddy. Not one of them
That yet looks on me, or would know me Ariel,
Fetch me the hat and rapier in my cell:
I will discase me, and myself present
As I was sometime Milan: quickly, spirit;
Thou shalt ere long be free.

THE TEMPEST (ACT 1 SCENE 2)

(Write your answers on a separate piece of paper.)

1 **a)** How does Shakespeare present the relationship between Prospero and Ariel in this extract? (15 marks)

b) How does Shakespeare present the relationship between Prospero and Ariel in the play as a whole? (15 marks)

2 How does Shakespeare present the theme of power in the play as a whole? (30 marks)

At this point in the play, Prospero has been checking that Ariel created the storm exactly as ordered.

PROSPERO	Ariel, thy charge Exactly is perform'd: but there's more work. What is the time o' the day?
ARIEL	Past the mid season.
PROSPERO	At least two glasses. The time 'twixt six and now Must by us both be spent most preciously.
ARIEL	Is there more toil? Since thou dost give me pains, Let me remember thee what thou hast promised, Which is not yet perform'd me.
PROSPERO	How now? moody? What is't thou canst demand?
ARIEL	My liberty.
PROSPERO	Before the time be out? no more!
ARIEL	I prithee, Remember I have done thee worthy service; Told thee no lies, made thee no mistakings, served Without or grudge or grumblings: thou didst promise To bate me a full year.
PROSPERO	Dost thou forget From what a torment I did free thee?
ARIEL	No.
PROSPERO	Thou dost, and think'st it much to tread the ooze Of the salt deep, To run upon the sharp wind of the north, To do me business in the veins o' the earth When it is baked with frost.
ARIEL	I do not, sir.
PROSPERO	Thou liest, malignant thing! Hast thou forgot The foul witch Sycorax, who with age and envy Was grown into a hoop? hast thou forgot her?
ARIEL	No, sir.
PROSPERO	Thou hast. Where was she born? speak; tell me.
ARIEL	Sir, in Argier.
PROSPERO	O, was she so? I must Once in a month recount what thou hast been, Which thou forget'st.

For more help on this topic, see Letts GCSE English Revision Guide pages 58–68.

Shakespeare

TWELFTH NIGHT (ACT 1 SCENE 1)

(Write your answers on a separate piece of paper.)

1 **a)** How does Shakespeare present Orsino's love for Olivia in this extract? (15 marks)

b) How does Shakespeare present Orsino and Olivia's relationship in the play as a whole? (15 marks)

2 How does Shakespeare present different types of love in the play as a whole? (30 marks)

At the start of the play, we meet Duke Orsino; he is in love with Olivia but she will not return his love.

DUKE ORSINO	If music be the food of love, play on;
	Give me excess of it, that, surfeiting,
	The appetite may sicken, and so die.
	That strain again! it had a dying fall:
	O, it came o'er my ear like the sweet sound,
	That breathes upon a bank of violets,
	Stealing and giving odour! Enough; no more:
	'Tis not so sweet now as it was before.
	O spirit of love! how quick and fresh art thou,
	That, notwithstanding thy capacity
	Receiveth as the sea, nought enters there,
	Of what validity and pitch soe'er,
	But falls into abatement and low price,
	Even in a minute: so full of shapes is fancy
	That it alone is high fantastical.
CURIO	Will you go hunt, my lord?
DUKE ORSINO	What, Curio?
CURIO	The hart.
DUKE ORSINO	Why, so I do, the noblest that I have:
	O, when mine eyes did see Olivia first,
	Methought she purged the air of pestilence!
	That instant was I turn'd into a hart;
	And my desires, like fell and cruel hounds,
	E'er since pursue me.
	*(Enter **Valentine**)*
	How now! what news from her?
VALENTINE	So please my lord, I might not be admitted;
	But from her handmaid do return this answer:
	The element itself, till seven years' heat,
	Shall not behold her face at ample view;
	But, like a cloistress, she will veiled walk
	And water once a day her chamber round
	With eye-offending brine: all this to season
	A brother's dead love, which she would keep fresh
	And lasting in her sad remembrance.

TWELFTH NIGHT (ACT 2 SCENE 3)

(Write your answers on a separate piece of paper.)

1 **a)** How does Shakespeare present the character of Malvolio in this extract? (15 marks)

b) How does Shakespeare present Malvolio in the play as a whole? (15 marks)

2 How does Shakespeare present the theme of ambition in the play as a whole? (30 marks)

At this point in the play, Malvolio arrives to tell Sir Toby off for the drunken noise he is making in Olivia's house.

*(Enter **Malvolio**)*

MALVOLIO My masters, are you mad? or what are you? Have ye no wit, manners, nor honesty, but to gabble like tinkers at this time of night? Do ye make an alehouse of my lady's house, that ye squeak out your coziers' catches without any mitigation or remorse of voice? Is there no respect of place, persons, nor time in you?

SIR TOBY BELCH We did keep time, sir, in our catches. Sneck up!

MALVOLIO Sir Toby, I must be round with you. My lady bade me tell you, that, though she harbours you as her kinsman, she's nothing allied to your disorders. If you can separate yourself and your misdemeanors, you are welcome to the house; if not, an it would please you to take leave of her, she is very willing to bid you farewell.

SIR TOBY BELCH *(Sings)* 'Farewell, dear heart, since I must needs be gone.'

MARIA Nay, good Sir Toby.

CLOWN *(Sings)* 'His eyes do show his days are almost done.'

MALVOLIO Is't even so?

SIR TOBY BELCH *(Sings)* 'But I will never die.'

CLOWN *(Sings)* Sir Toby, there you lie.

MALVOLIO This is much credit to you.

SIR TOBY BELCH *(Sings)* 'Shall I bid him go?'

CLOWN *(Sings)* 'What an if you do?'

SIR TOBY BELCH *(Sings)* 'Shall I bid him go, and spare not?'

Clown *(Sings)* 'O no, no, no, no, you dare not.'

SIR TOBY BELCH Out o' tune, sir: ye lie. Art any more than a steward? Dost thou think, because thou art virtuous, there shall be no more cakes and ale?

CLOWN Yes, by Saint Anne, and ginger shall be hot i' the mouth too.

SIR TOBY BELCH Thou'rt i' the right. Go, sir, rub your chain with crumbs. A stoup of wine, Maria!

MALVOLIO Mistress Mary, if you prized my lady's favour at any thing more than contempt, you would not give means for this uncivil rule: she shall know of it, by this hand.

(Exit)

For more help on this topic, see Letts GCSE English Revision Guide pages 58–68.

Shakespeare

JULIUS CAESAR (ACT 1 SCENE 2)
(Write your answers on a separate piece of paper.)

1 **a)** How does Shakespeare present the character of Julius Caesar in this extract? (15 marks)

b) How does Shakespeare present Julius Caesar in the play as a whole? (15 marks)

2 How does Shakespeare present the theme of power in the play as a whole?

(30 marks)

At this point in the play, Julius Caesar is making his way through the streets to the Forum.

*(Flourish. Enter **Caesar**; **Antony**, for the course; **Calpurnia, Portia, Decius Brutus, Cicero, Brutus, Cassius,** and **Casca**; a great crowd following, among them a Soothsayer)*

CAESAR	Calpurnia!
CASCA	Peace, ho! Caesar speaks.
CAESAR	Calpurnia!
CALPURNIA	Here, my lord.
CAESAR	Stand you directly in Antonius' way,
	When he doth run his course. Antonius!
ANTONY	Caesar, my lord?
CAESAR	Forget not, in your speed, Antonius,
	To touch Calpurnia; for our elders say,
	The barren, touched in this holy chase,
	Shake off their sterile curse.
ANTONY	I shall remember:
	When Caesar says 'do this,' it is perform'd.
CAESAR	Set on; and leave no ceremony out.
	(Flourish)
SOOTHSAYER	Caesar!
CAESAR	Ha! who calls?
CASCA	Bid every noise be still: peace yet again!
CAESAR	Who is it in the press that calls on me?
	I hear a tongue, shriller than all the music,
	Cry 'Caesar!' Speak; Caesar is turn'd to hear.
SOOTHSAYER	Beware the ides of March.
CAESAR	What man is that?
BRUTUS	A soothsayer bids you beware the ides of March.
CAESAR	Set him before me; let me see his face.
CASSIUS	Fellow, come from the throng; look upon Caesar.
CAESAR	What say'st thou to me now? speak once again.
SOOTHSAYER	Beware the ides of March.
CAESAR	He is a dreamer; let us leave him: pass.

56 Shakespeare

JULIUS CAESAR (ACT 3 SCENE 3)

(Write your answers on a separate piece of paper.)

1 a) How does Shakespeare present the character of Antony is this extract?   (15 marks)

   b) How does Shakespeare present Antony in the play as a whole?   (15 marks)

2 How does Shakespeare present the theme of manipulation in the play as a whole?   (30 marks)

At this point in the play, the conspirators have come to the Forum to explain their reasons for assassinating Caesar. After Brutus's speech, Antony arrives with Caesar's body.

> **ANTONY**   Friends, Romans, countrymen, lend me your ears;
> I come to bury Caesar, not to praise him.
> The evil that men do lives after them;
> The good is oft interred with their bones;
> So let it be with Caesar. The noble Brutus
> Hath told you Caesar was ambitious:
> If it were so, it was a grievous fault,
> And grievously hath Caesar answer'd it.
> Here, under leave of Brutus and the rest--
> For Brutus is an honourable man;
> So are they all, all honourable men--
> Come I to speak in Caesar's funeral.
> He was my friend, faithful and just to me:
> But Brutus says he was ambitious;
> And Brutus is an honourable man.
> He hath brought many captives home to Rome
> Whose ransoms did the general coffers fill:
> Did this in Caesar seem ambitious?
> When that the poor have cried, Caesar hath wept:
> Ambition should be made of sterner stuff:
> Yet Brutus says he was ambitious;
> And Brutus is an honourable man.
> You all did see that on the Lupercal
> I thrice presented him a kingly crown,
> Which he did thrice refuse: was this ambition?
> Yet Brutus says he was ambitious;
> And, sure, he is an honourable man.
> I speak not to disprove what Brutus spoke,
> But here I am to speak what I do know.
> You all did love him once, not without cause:
> What cause withholds you then, to mourn for him?
> O judgment! thou art fled to brutish beasts,
> And men have lost their reason. Bear with me;
> My heart is in the coffin there with Caesar,
> And I must pause till it come back to me.

For more help on this topic, see Letts GCSE English Revision Guide pages 58–68.

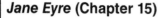

Jane Eyre (Chapter 15)

(Write your answers on a separate piece of paper.)

1 **a)** How does Brontë present Jane as a vulnerable, frightened character in this extract? (15 marks)

b) How does Brontë present the vulnerable and frightened side of Jane's character in the novel as a whole? (15 marks)

2 **a)** How does Brontë create an atmosphere of mystery in this extract? (15 marks)

b) How does Brontë create an atmosphere of mystery in the novel as a whole? (15 marks)

At this point in the novel, Jane is living and working at Thornfield.

I hardly know whether I had slept or not after this musing; at any rate, I started wide awake on hearing a vague murmur, peculiar and lugubrious, which sounded, I thought, just above me. I wished I had kept my candle burning: the night was drearily dark; my spirits were depressed. I rose and sat up in bed, listening. The sound was hushed.

I tried again to sleep; but my heart beat anxiously: my inward tranquillity was broken. The clock, far down in the hall, struck two. Just then it seemed my chamber-door was touched; as if fingers had swept the panels in groping a way along the dark gallery outside. I said, "Who is there?" Nothing answered. I was chilled with fear.

All at once I remembered that it might be Pilot, who, when the kitchen-door chanced to be left open, not unfrequently found his way up to the threshold of Mr. Rochester's chamber: I had seen him lying there myself in the mornings. The idea calmed me somewhat: I lay down. Silence composes the nerves; and as an unbroken hush now reigned again through the whole house, I began to feel the return of slumber. But it was not fated that I should sleep that night. A dream had scarcely approached my ear, when it fled affrighted, scared by a marrow-freezing incident enough.

This was a demoniac laugh—low, suppressed, and deep—uttered, as it seemed, at the very keyhole of my chamber door. The head of my bed was near the door, and I thought at first the goblin-laugher stood at my bedside—or rather, crouched by my pillow: but I rose, looked round, and could see nothing; while, as I still gazed, the unnatural sound was reiterated: and I knew it came from behind the panels. My first impulse was to rise and fasten the bolt; my next, again to cry out, "Who is there?"

Something gurgled and moaned. Ere long, steps retreated up the gallery towards the third-storey staircase: a door had lately been made to shut in that staircase; I heard it open and close, and all was still.

Great Expectations (Chapter 29)

(Write your answers on a separate piece of paper.)

1 **a)** How does Dickens present the character of Estella as unfeeling in this extract?   (15 marks)

 b) How does Dickens present Estella as unfeeling in the novel as a whole?   (15 marks)

2 **a)** How does Dickens present Pip's love for Estella in this extract?   (15 marks)

 b) How does Dickens present Pip's love for Estella in the novel as a whole?   (15 marks)

At this point in the novel, Pip has travelled from London to see his family. He visits Miss Havisham and meets Estella, who he has not seen for a long time.

The air of completeness and superiority with which she walked at my side, and the air of youthfulness and submission with which I walked at hers, made a contrast that I strongly felt. It would have rankled in me more than it did, if I had not regarded myself as eliciting it by being so set apart for her and assigned to her.

The garden was too overgrown and rank for walking in with ease, and after we had made the round of it twice or thrice, we came out again into the brewery yard. I showed her to a nicety where I had seen her walking on the casks, that first old day, and she said, with a cold and careless look in that direction, "Did I?" I reminded her where she had come out of the house and given me my meat and drink, and she said, "I don't remember." "Not remember that you made me cry?" said I. "No," said she, and shook her head and looked about her. I verily believe that her not remembering and not minding in the least, made me cry again, inwardly,—and that is the sharpest crying of all.

"You must know," said Estella, condescending to me as a brilliant and beautiful woman might, "that I have no heart,—if that has anything to do with my memory."

I got through some jargon to the effect that I took the liberty of doubting that. That I knew better. That there could be no such beauty without it.

"Oh! I have a heart to be stabbed in or shot in, I have no doubt," said Estella, "and of course if it ceased to beat I should cease to be. But you know what I mean. I have no softness there, no—sympathy—sentiment—nonsense."

What was it that was borne in upon my mind when she stood still and looked attentively at me? Anything that I had seen in Miss Havisham? No. In some of her looks and gestures there was that tinge of resemblance to Miss Havisham which may often be noticed to have been acquired by children, from a grown person with whom they have been much associated and secluded, and which, when childhood is passed, will produce a remarkable occasional likeness of expression between faces that are otherwise quite different. And yet I could not trace this to Miss Havisham. I looked again, and though she was still looking at me, the suggestion was gone.

What was it?

"I am serious," said Estella, not so much with a frown (for her brow was smooth) as with a darkening of her face; "if we are to be thrown much together, you had better believe it at once. No!" imperiously stopping me as I opened my lips. "I have not bestowed my tenderness anywhere. I have never had any such thing."

For more help on this topic, see Letts GCSE English Revision Guide pages 72–78.

***The Strange Case of Dr Jekyll and Mr Hyde* (Dr Jekyll's Full Statement Of The Case)**
(Write your answers on a separate piece of paper.)

1 **a)** How does Stevenson present how Dr Jekyll struggles with his Mr Hyde
persona in this extract? (15 marks)

   b) How does Stevenson present how Dr Jekyll struggles with his Mr Hyde
persona in the novel as a whole? (15 marks)

2 **a)** How does Stevenson present Mr Hyde as monstrous in this extract? (15 marks)

   b) How does Stevenson present Mr Hyde as monstrous in the novel
as a whole? (15 marks)

At this point in the novel, Dr Jekyll is explaining, in his statement, how the transformations into Mr Hyde became unwanted and difficult to control.

I was stepping leisurely across the court after breakfast, drinking the chill of the air with pleasure, when I was seized again with those indescribable sensations that heralded the change; and I had but the time to gain the shelter of my cabinet, before I was once again raging and freezing with the passions of Hyde. It took on this occasion a double dose to recall me to myself; and alas! Six hours after, as I sat looking sadly in the fire, the pangs returned, and the drug had to be re-administered.

In short, from that day forth it seemed only by a great effort as of gymnastics, and only under the immediate stimulation of the drug, that I was able to wear the countenance of Jekyll. At all hours of the day and night, I would be taken with the premonitory shudder; above all, if I slept, or even dozed for a moment in my chair, it was always as Hyde that I awakened. Under the strain of this continually-impending doom and by the sleeplessness to which I now condemned myself, ay, even beyond what I had thought possible to man, I became, in my own person, a creature eaten up and emptied by fever, languidly weak both in body and mind, and solely occupied by one thought: the horror of my other self. But when I slept, or when the virtue of the medicine wore off, I would leap almost without transition (for the pangs of transformation grew daily less marked) into the possession of a fancy brimming with images of terror, a soul boiling with causeless hatreds, and a body that seemed not strong enough to contain the raging energies of life. The powers of Hyde seemed to have grown with the sickliness of Jekyll. And certainly the hate that now divided them was equal on each side. With Jekyll, it was a thing of vital instinct. He had now seen the full deformity of that creature that shared with him some of the phenomena of consciousness, and was co-heir with him to death: and beyond these links of community, which in themselves made the most poignant part of his distress, he thought of Hyde, for all his energy of life, as of something not only hellish but inorganic. This was the shocking thing; that the slime of the pit seemed to utter cries and voices; that the amorphous dust gesticulated and sinned; that what was dead, and had no shape, should usurp the offices of life.

And this again, that that insurgent horror was knit to him closer than a wife, closer than an eye; lay caged in his flesh, where he heard it mutter and felt it struggle to be born; and at every hour of weakness, and in the confidence of slumber, prevailed against him and deposed him out of life.

Pride and Prejudice (Chapter 3)

(Write your answers on a separate piece of paper.)

1 **a)** How does Austen present the character of Mr Darcy as dislikeable in this extract? (15 marks)
    b) How does Austen develop the character of Mr Darcy in the novel as a whole? (15 marks)

2 **a)** How does Austen present the theme of class and manners in this extract? (15 marks)
    b) How does Austen present the theme of class and manners in the novel as a whole? (15 marks)

At this point in the novel, the Bennett family meet Mr Bingley and his friend Mr Darcy at a ball.

Mr. Bingley was good-looking and gentlemanlike; he had a pleasant countenance, and easy, unaffected manners. His sisters were fine women, with an air of decided fashion. His brother-in-law, Mr. Hurst, merely looked the gentleman; but his friend Mr. Darcy soon drew the attention of the room by his fine, tall person, handsome features, noble mien, and the report which was in general circulation within five minutes after his entrance, of his having ten thousand a year. The gentlemen pronounced him to be a fine figure of a man, the ladies declared he was much handsomer than Mr. Bingley, and he was looked at with great admiration for about half the evening, till his manners gave a disgust which turned the tide of his popularity; for he was discovered to be proud; to be above his company, and above being pleased; and not all his large estate in Derbyshire could then save him from having a most forbidding, disagreeable countenance, and being unworthy to be compared with his friend.

Mr. Bingley had soon made himself acquainted with all the principal people in the room; he was lively and unreserved, danced every dance, was angry that the ball closed so early, and talked of giving one himself at Netherfield. Such amiable qualities must speak for themselves. What a contrast between him and his friend! Mr. Darcy danced only once with Mrs. Hurst and once with Miss Bingley, declined being introduced to any other lady, and spent the rest of the evening in walking about the room, speaking occasionally to one of his own party. His character was decided. He was the proudest, most disagreeable man in the world, and everybody hoped that he would never come there again. Amongst the most violent against him was Mrs. Bennet, whose dislike of his general behaviour was sharpened into particular resentment by his having slighted one of her daughters.

Elizabeth Bennet had been obliged, by the scarcity of gentlemen, to sit down for two dances; and during part of that time, Mr. Darcy had been standing near enough for her to hear a conversation between him and Mr. Bingley, who came from the dance for a few minutes, to press his friend to join it.

"Come, Darcy," said he, "I must have you dance. I hate to see you standing about by yourself in this stupid manner. You had much better dance."

"I certainly shall not. You know how I detest it, unless I am particularly acquainted with my partner. At such an assembly as this it would be insupportable. Your sisters are engaged, and there is not another woman in the room whom it would not be a punishment to me to stand up with."

"I would not be so fastidious as you are," cried Mr. Bingley, "for a kingdom! Upon my honour, I never met with so many pleasant girls in my life as I have this evening; and there are several of them you see uncommonly pretty."

"You are dancing with the only handsome girl in the room," said Mr. Darcy, looking at the eldest Miss Bennet.

"Oh! She is the most beautiful creature I ever beheld! But there is one of her sisters sitting down just behind you, who is very pretty, and I dare say very agreeable. Do let me ask my partner to introduce you."

"Which do you mean?" and turning round he looked for a moment at Elizabeth, till catching her eye, he withdrew his own and coldly said: "She is tolerable, but not handsome enough to tempt me; I am in no humour at present to give consequence to young ladies who are slighted by other men. You had better return to your partner and enjoy her smiles, for you are wasting your time with me."

For more help on this topic, see Letts GCSE English Revision Guide pages 72–78.

A Christmas Carol (Stave One)
(Write your answers on a separate piece of paper.)

1 **a)** How does Dickens present the character of Scrooge as dislikeable in this extract? (15 marks)

b) How does Dickens present the character of Scrooge as dislikeable in the story as a whole? (15 marks)

2 **a)** How does Dickens present poverty in this extract? (15 marks)

b) How does Dickens present poverty and create sympathy within the reader in the story as a whole? (15 marks)

At this point in the story, Scrooge receives two visitors in his counting-house.

"Scrooge and Marley's, I believe," said one of the gentlemen, referring to his list. "Have I the pleasure of addressing Mr. Scrooge, or Mr. Marley?"

"Mr. Marley has been dead these seven years," Scrooge replied. "He died seven years ago, this very night."

"We have no doubt his liberality is well represented by his surviving partner," said the gentleman, presenting his credentials.

It certainly was; for they had been two kindred spirits. At the ominous word "liberality," Scrooge frowned, and shook his head, and handed the credentials back.

"At this festive season of the year, Mr. Scrooge," said the gentleman, taking up a pen, "it is more than usually desirable that we should make some slight provision for the Poor and destitute, who suffer greatly at the present time. Many thousands are in want of common necessaries; hundreds of thousands are in want of common comforts, sir."

"Are there no prisons?" asked Scrooge.

"Plenty of prisons," said the gentleman, laying down the pen again.

"And the Union workhouses?" demanded Scrooge. "Are they still in operation?"

"They are. Still," returned the gentleman, "I wish I could say they were not."

"The Treadmill and the Poor Law are in full vigour, then?" said Scrooge.

"Both very busy, sir."

"Oh! I was afraid, from what you said at first, that something had occurred to stop them in their useful course," said Scrooge. "I'm very glad to hear it."

"Under the impression that they scarcely furnish Christian cheer of mind or body to the multitude," returned the gentleman, "a few of us are endeavouring to raise a fund to buy the Poor some meat and drink, and means of warmth. We choose this time, because it is a time, of all others, when Want is keenly felt, and Abundance rejoices. What shall I put you down for?"

"Nothing!" Scrooge replied.

"You wish to be anonymous?"

"I wish to be left alone," said Scrooge. "Since you ask me what I wish, gentlemen, that is my answer. I don't make merry myself at Christmas and I can't afford to make idle people merry. I help to support the establishments I have mentioned – they cost enough; and those who are badly off must go there."

"Many can't go there; and many would rather die."

"If they would rather die," said Scrooge, "they had better do it, and decrease the surplus population."

Frankenstein (Chapter 16)

(Write your answers on a separate piece of paper.)

1 **a)** How does Shelley present the character of the Creature as desperately unhappy in this extract? (15 marks)

    b) How does Shelley present the Creature as desperately unhappy and create sympathy within the reader in the novel as a whole? (15 marks)

2 **a)** How does Shelley present the Creature's violent side in this extract? (15 marks)

    b) How does Shelley present the Creature's violent side in the novel as a whole? (15 marks)

At this point in the novel, the Creature describes to Victor Frankenstein his feelings at being driven from the cottage by Felix.

"Cursed, cursed creator! Why did I live? Why, in that instant, did I not extinguish the spark of existence which you had so wantonly bestowed? I know not; despair had not yet taken possession of me; my feelings were those of rage and revenge. I could with pleasure have destroyed the cottage and its inhabitants and have glutted myself with their shrieks and misery.

"When night came I quitted my retreat and wandered in the wood; and now, no longer restrained by the fear of discovery, I gave vent to my anguish in fearful howlings. I was like a wild beast that had broken the toils, destroying the objects that obstructed me and ranging through the wood with a stag-like swiftness. Oh! What a miserable night I passed! The cold stars shone in mockery, and the bare trees waved their branches above me; now and then the sweet voice of a bird burst forth amidst the universal stillness. All, save I, were at rest or in enjoyment; I, like the arch-fiend, bore a hell within me, and finding myself unsympathized with, wished to tear up the trees, spread havoc and destruction around me, and then to have sat down and enjoyed the ruin.

"But this was a luxury of sensation that could not endure; I became fatigued with excess of bodily exertion and sank on the damp grass in the sick impotence of despair. There was none among the myriads of men that existed who would pity or assist me; and should I feel kindness towards my enemies? No; from that moment I declared everlasting war against the species, and more than all, against him who had formed me and sent me forth to this insupportable misery.

"The sun rose; I heard the voices of men and knew that it was impossible to return to my retreat during that day. Accordingly I hid myself in some thick underwood, determining to devote the ensuing hours to reflection on my situation.

"The pleasant sunshine and the pure air of day restored me to some degree of tranquillity; and when I considered what had passed at the cottage, I could not help believing that I had been too hasty in my conclusions. I had certainly acted imprudently. It was apparent that my conversation had interested the father in my behalf, and I was a fool in having exposed my person to the horror of his children. I ought to have familiarized the old De Lacey to me, and by degrees to have discovered myself to the rest of his family, when they should have been prepared for my approach. But I did not believe my errors to be irretrievable, and after much consideration I resolved to return to the cottage, seek the old man, and by my representations win him to my party.

For more help on this topic, see Letts GCSE English Revision Guide pages 72–78.

Modern Fiction

Drama: Revising Character

Remember to focus on how language, structure and form are used to convey meaning.
(All questions are worth 15 marks.)
(Write your answers on a separate piece of paper.)

A Taste of Honey

1 How does Delaney present Helen as a mother?

2 How does Delaney present Geoffrey as a social outcast?

3 How does Delaney present Jo and Geoffrey's relationship?

An Inspector Calls

1 How does Priestley present Mrs Birling?

2 How does Priestley develop the character of Eric Birling?

3 How does Priestley present and develop the relationship between Shiela and Gerald?

Blood Brothers

1 How does Russell present Mrs Johnstone as a mother?

2 How does Russell present the character of Linda?

3 How does Russell present the changes in the fortunes of Eddie and Mickey?

DNA

1 How does Kelly present the relationship between Phil and Lea?

2 How does Kelly show changes in the gang members?

3 How does Kelly present the characters of Jan and Mark?

History Boys

1 How does Bennett present the character of Scripps?

2 How does Bennett present the relationship between Hector and Dorothy?

3 How does Bennett present Posner as an outsider?

Hobson's Choice

1 How does Brighouse present Hobson as a father?

2 How does Brighouse present the relationship between Will and Maggie?

3 How does Brighouse present the characters of Alice and Vickey?

Journey's End

1 How does Sherriff present the relationship between Stanhope and Raleigh?

2 How does Sherriff present the relationship between Mason and Trotter?

3 How does Sherriff present the character of Osborne?

My Mother Said I Never Should

1 How does Keatley present the relationship between Jackie and Margaret?

2 How does Keatley present the relationship between Doris and Margaret?

3 How does Keatley present the character of Rosie?

The Curious Incident Of The Dog In The Night-Time

1 How does Stephens present Christopher's autism?

2 How does Stephens present the relationship between Christopher and his father?

3 How does Stephens present the character of Judy, Christopher's mother?

Generate Your Own Questions

➤ Choose any of the main characters in your play and analyse how they are presented by the writer (what are they like and how does the author show this?).

➤ Focus specifically on analysing how a character changes during the play.

➤ Choose two characters that are linked in the play and analyse how their relationship is presented.

For more help on this topic, see Letts GCSE English Revision Guide pages 80–81.

Drama: Revising Themes

Remember to focus on how language, structure and form are used to convey meaning.
(All questions are worth 15 marks.)
(Write your answers on a separate piece of paper.)

A Taste of Honey

1 How does Delaney explore social taboos in the play?

2 How does Delaney use the character of Jo to explore the theme of hopes and fears?

3 How does Delaney use Helen and Peter to explore the theme of gender?

An Inspector Calls

1 How does Priestley use the Inspector to explore the theme of judgement?

2 How does Priestley use Mr Birling to explore the theme of class?

3 How does Priestley use the setting of the house to explore his ideas?

Blood Brothers

1 How does Russell use different times to explore his ideas?

2 How does Russell explore the theme of brotherhood?

3 How does Russell explore different social problems?

DNA

1 How does Kelly use the character of Adam to explore the theme of bullying?

2 How does Kelly explore the theme of leadership?

3 How does Kelly make use of monologues?

History Boys

1 How does Bennett use Dakin to explore the theme of attraction?

2 How does Bennett explore different ideas about education?

3 How does Bennett explore the theme of women?

Hobson's Choice

1 How does Brighouse use Maggie to explore the theme of women?

2 How does Brighouse explore the theme of marriage?

3 How does Brighouse explore the theme of money?

Journey's End

1 How does Sherriff use the character of Stanhope to explore the effects of war?

2 How does Sherriff explore the theme of duty?

3 How does Sherriff use the trench setting to explore his ideas?

My Mother Said I Never Should

1 How does Keatley explore the theme of growing up?

2 How does Keatley use time to explore her ideas?

3 How does Keatley explore the theme of independence?

The Curious Incident of the Dog in the Night-Time

1 How does Stephens use Christopher to explore the theme of rules?

2 How does Stephens explore the theme of parents?

3 How does Stephens explore the theme of communication?

Generate Your Own Questions

➤ Choose any of the main themes in your play and analyse how they are explored by the writer (what ideas does the author have about the theme and how are these conveyed to the audience?).

➤ Focus specifically on analysing how a character presents a certain theme in the play.

➤ Analyse the settings (place and/or time) or stage directions within your play and how the writer uses them to get across different ideas.

For more help on this topic, see Letts GCSE English Revision Guide pages 82–83.

Prose: Revising Character

Remember to focus on how language, structure and form are used to convey meaning.
(All questions are worth 15 marks.)
(Write your answers on a separate piece of paper.)

The Lord of the Flies

1 How does Golding present the relationship between Ralph and Jack?

2 How does Golding present the relationship between Ralph and Piggy?

3 How does Golding present the character of Simon?

Animal Farm

1 How does Orwell present the differences between Snowball and Napoleon?

2 How does Orwell present the character of Benjamin?

3 How does Orwell present Boxer as a figure of inspiration on the farm?

Never Let Me Go

1 How does Ishiguro present the relationship between Kathy and Tommy?

2 How does Ishiguro present the character of Madame?

3 How does Ishiguro develop the character of Ruth?

Anita and Me

1 How does Syal present the relationship between Meena and Anita?

2 How does Syal present the character of Sam?

3 How does Syal present the relationship between Mama and Papa?

The Woman in Black

1 How does Hill present the ways that Arthur changes?

2 How does Hill present the character of Sam Daily?

3 How does Hill present and use the characters of Jerome and the Landlord?

Pigeon English

1 How does Kelman present the relationship between Harri and Dean?

2 How does Kelman present the ways in which Harri changes?

3 How does Kelman present the character of Harri's mother?

Generate Your Own Questions

➤ Choose any of the main characters in your novel and analyse how they are presented by the writer (what are they like and how does the author show this?).

➤ Focus specifically on analysing how a character changes during the novel.

➤ Choose two characters that are linked in the novel and analyse how their relationship is presented.

For more help on this topic, see Letts GCSE English Revision Guide pages 80–81.

Prose: Revising Themes

Remember to focus on how language, structure and form are used to convey meaning. (All questions are worth 15 marks.)
(Write your answers on a separate piece of paper.)

The Lord Of The Flies

1 How does Golding explore the theme of law and order?

2 How does Golding use Ralph and Jack to explore the theme of leadership?

3 How does Golding explore the theme of fear?

Animal Farm

1 How does Orwell use the pigs to explore the theme of corruption?

2 How does Orwell explore the theme of government?

3 How does Orwell explore the theme of freedom and independence?

Never Let Me Go

1 How does Ishiguro use Kathy, Ruth and Tommy to explore the theme of hopes and dreams?

2 How does Ishiguro explore the theme of not having freedom?

3 How does Ishiguro use place and time to explore different ideas?

Anita and Me

1 How does Syal explore the theme of growing up?

2 How does Syal explore the clash between conformity and independence?

3 How does Syal explore the importance of cultural heritage?

The Woman in Black

1 How does Hill explore the theme of fear?

2 How does Hill use places in the novel?

3 How does Hill explore the theme of loss?

Pigeon English

1 How does Kelman use Harri to explore the theme of right and wrong?

2 How does Kelman explore the theme of social problems?

3 How does Kelman explore the theme of growing up?

Generate Your Own Questions

➤ Choose any of the main themes in your novel and analyse how they are explored by the writer (what ideas does the author have about the theme and how are these conveyed to the reader?).

➤ Focus specifically on analysing how a character presents a certain theme in the play.

➤ Analyse the settings (place and/or time) or the narrative structure within your novel and how the writer uses them to get across different ideas.

For more help on this topic, see Letts GCSE English Revision Guide pages 82–83.

Practice Paper A GCSE English Language

Paper 1: Explorations in Creative Reading and Writing

Time allowed: 1 hour 45 minutes

You are advised to spend 15 minutes reading through the source and the questions before you begin writing.

Section A: Reading

Answer all the questions in this section.
You are advised to spend about 45 minutes on this section.
(Write your answers to the questions on a separate piece of paper.)

1 Read again the second paragraph of the source. List four things from this part of the text that the narrator is grateful for.

(4 marks)

2 Look in detail at the first paragraph of the source. How does the writer use language and sentence structure here to describe different feelings? You could include the writer's choice of:
- words and phrases
- language features and techniques
- sentence forms.

(8 marks)

3 You now need to think about the whole of the source. The text is from the opening of a novel. How has the writer structured the text to interest you as a reader? You could write about:
- what the writer focuses your attention on in different paragraphs
- what information the writer holds back
- any other structural features that interest you.

(8 marks)

4 Use the whole of the source to answer this question.
A student, having read this novel opening, said: 'The writer really brings the narrator to life. You can understand her; you feel like she's talking directly to you and confiding in you.'
To what extent do you agree? In your response, you should:
- write about your own impression of the narrator
- evaluate how the writer has created these impressions
- support your opinions with quotations from the text.

(20 marks)

Source

This extract is the opening of a novel by Carol Shields. Published in 2002, it explores how the life of Reta Winters changes. She is a successful writer with a happy family and good friends until, one day, her eldest daughter suddenly drops out of university and stops speaking to anyone.

'Unless' by Carol Shields

IT HAPPENS THAT I am going through a period of great unhappiness and loss just now. All my life I've heard people speak of finding themselves in acute pain, bankrupt in spirit and body, but I've never understood what they meant. To lose. To have lost. I believed these visitations of darkness lasted only a few minutes or hours and that these saddened people, in between bouts, were occupied, as we all were, with the useful monotony of happiness. But happiness is not what I thought. Happiness is the lucky pane of glass you carry in your head. It takes all your cunning just to hang on to it, and once it's smashed you have to move into a different sort of life.

In my new life—the summer of the year 2000—I am attempting to "count my blessings." Everyone I know advises me to take up this repellent strategy, as though they really believe a dramatic loss can be replaced by the renewed appreciation of all one has been given. I have a husband, Tom, who loves me and is faithful to me and is very decent looking as well, tallish, thin, and losing his hair nicely. We live in a house with a paid-up mortgage, and our house is set in the prosperous rolling hills of Ontario, only an hour's drive north of Toronto. Two of our three daughters, Natalie, fifteen, and Christine, sixteen, live at home. They are intelligent and lively and attractive and loving, though they too have shared in the loss, as has Tom.

And I have my writing.

"You have your writing!" friends say. A murmuring chorus: But you have your writing, Reta. No one is crude enough to suggest that my sorrow will eventually become material for my writing, but probably they think it.

And it's true. There is a curious and faintly distasteful comfort, at the age of forty-three, forty-four in September, in contemplating what I have managed to write and publish during those impossibly childish and sunlit days before I understood the meaning of grief. "My Writing": this is a very small poultice to hold up against my damaged self, but better, I have been persuaded, than no comfort at all.

Section B: Writing

Answer one question from this section.
You are advised to spend 45 minutes on this section.
Write in full sentences.
You are reminded of the need to plan your answer.
You should leave enough time to check your work at the end.
(Write your answer on a separate piece of paper.)

5 You are going to enter a creative writing competition.
Either:

a) Write a description suggested by this picture:

Or:

b) Write the opening part of a story that conveys powerful emotions.

(24 marks for content and organisation / 16 marks for technical accuracy.)

Practice Paper B GCSE English Language

Paper 2: Writers' Viewpoints and Perspectives

Time allowed: 1 hour 45 minutes

You are advised to spend 15 minutes reading through the sources and the questions before you begin writing.

Section A: Reading
Answer all the questions in this section.
You are advised to spend about 45 minutes on this section.
(Write your answers to the questions on a separate piece of paper.)

1 Re-read the last two paragraphs of Source A. Choose four of the following statements that are true:

a) Tom Baker thinks it was strange, during a war, to ask children what they want to be when they grow up. ☐

b) Children never answered when they were asked what they wanted to be. ☐

c) People liked to hear a child say he would look after his mother. ☐

d) Tom Baker used to pray to be an orphan. ☐

e) The local pub was called the Red Lion. ☐

f) Tom Baker always talks politely to children when he meets them. ☐

g) Tate and Lyle's was the name of the local supermarket. ☐

h) Tom Baker's tone is quite jokey. ☐

(4 marks)

2 You need to refer to Source A and Source B for this question. Using details from both sources, write a summary of the writers' attitudes about death. **(8 marks)**

3 You now need to refer only to Source B. Looking at the second paragraph, how does Admiral Heath use language to convey his experience of war? **(12 marks)**

4 For this question, you need to refer to the whole of Source A together with Source B. Compare how the two writers convey their different attitudes to war.
- Compare their different attitudes.
- Compare the methods they use to convey their attitudes.
- Support your ideas with quotations from both texts. **(16 marks)**

Source A

This is an extract from 'Who On Earth Is Tom Baker?', the autobiography of the actor Tom Baker. Published in 1997, this extract describes his childhood during World War Two and his unusual ambition.

My first ambition was to be an orphan. During the war of 1939-45, Liverpool was a good place to be. All routine was broken by the fear of death from the Germans' bombs. The pleasure of being a child at that time is not easy to describe without seeming flippant. But it was drama, high drama: fires at night, the fires that burned people's houses down; bombs fell and left exotically shaped fragments in the form of shrapnel. And we collected it and traded it. As long as we were not hurt - and I wasn't - life seemed wonderful. At the gasworks one night a landmine, which was a bomb on a parachute, had descended gently and was hanging from one of the arms of the gasometer. Hundreds of people gathered and stood around, conjecturing about the size of the bomb. Bets were placed. The police and the fire brigade tried to get the people clear of the scene and, with difficulty, did so. Grumbling and arguing people were forced away from the danger area bitterly resenting the bossiness of the authorities.

Policemen and air-raid wardens and fire watchers loved the power they had to shout at their neighbours and tell them what to do, and they exercised it. In the shelters we sat all night or until the 'All Clear'. And people talked and talked and prayed and prayed that God would spare us. We were convinced, like all good Christians, that God was on our side.

The advantage of being an orphan sprang from the generosity of the American people. If your Dad or Mam was blown up then you really got some attention. Presents would arrive from America with a nice card from the President himself: funny hats and jackets that were considered very smart. At that time, the Superman comics were widely read and there were American soldiers all over the place. As American accents only reached us through the films, it was like being in a movie to meet them or to wear clothes that came from their country. We adored everything about America. We just could not get enough of it, from gum to caps to tee shirts with funny figures printed on them. We even copied the way the Americans walked, though Father Leonard, our parish priest, didn't like that bit of admiration. He disapproved of rolling buttocks.

The only drawback was that to qualify for the goodies your Mam had to be in Heaven. So I prayed hard that a bomb would drop on mine as she trudged home from the Sefton Arms.

It was common in those days for adults to ask quite small children what they wanted to be when they grew up. What a question in the middle of a world war! You can't ask that question now because it would be tactless as so many children are not going to become anything at all. But then everybody seemed to be asking children what their future would be. As if a child might know. These days when I see a child in Waitrose and smile and say, 'Hello, are you going to visit your Mum in her sheltered accommodation when you grow up?' it provokes glistening eyes and hollow laughter. And if you pursue it with, 'Or are you going to be a drugs dealer?' it may result in a snub. But in the days I'm talking about such enquiries were quite commonplace. Of course there was also a repertoire of stock answers from the child. One might answer: 'I'm going into the Merchant Navy, or the foreign missionaries, or the Adelphi Hotel, or Tate and Lyle's sugar factory' or, best of all, 'I'm going to stay at home with me Mam and look after her.' I don't know which precocious little sod first said that but the phrase passed into the language and made hard, sceptical men nod and bow their heads and strong, good-living women weep. It often led to a hug of such intensity that your nose would be broken. There were several broken-nosed five-year-olds in my school.

Source B

This is an extract from a letter by Admiral Sir Leopold George Heath KC, written during the Crimea War of 1853–56.

H.M.S. "Niger", May, 1854

May 13th. – One does not realise what war really is until one has either suffered oneself or seen its sad effects on one's friend. (...)

We saw the poor "Tiger" within thirty yards of the beach, over which rose cliffs a hundred and twenty feet high, crowned by no end of Russian field pieces and troops, the former shelling the "Tiger." We opened our fire as soon as we had got within range, but it was clear the "Tiger" was in the enemy's hands, for she had no colours up; she made no answer to my signal "How can I assist you?" and no return to the Russian guns, nor could we see anyone on board. The Russian fire was therefore probably intended to lure us to closer quarters, or perhaps to tempt our boats in to bring off the crew. However, Powell, the Commander of the "Vesuvius," came on board and said he thought he had seen the "Tiger's" crew marching up the hill side, and so as nothing more was to be done and there was no object in merely exchanging shots with the filed pieces, we steamed out of range and ceased firing. Smoke then began to rise from the "Tiger," and she was soon very soon in a blaze fore and aft; whether her own crew or the Russian shells had done it we don't know. In any case it was the best thing that could have happened, for with a garrison at Odessa of thirty thousand men and the ship thirty yards from the beach it would have been absurd to attempt and impossible to succeed in getting her off. I then hoisted a flag of truce and sent in a note to the Russian Commander asking for information about the crew. My boat was met half way by one from the shore, whose officer promised an answer should be sent, and explained (as well as a man speaking in Italian could to one who only understood English) that one officer (who turned out to be Captain Giffard) and one sailor were killed and three wounded, and that the rest were all prisoners, that the guns were all thrown overboard and the ship full of water. I waited for three hours, but no answer came. In the meantime the fire was doing its work, the masts fell in succession, and the whole of the upper works were in flames.

The poor "Tigers" seem to have done their best to get off, their boats were out and they had laid out a stern anchor and thrown their guns overboard; but it is difficult to account for their being all made prisoners, unless it was that they were so hard at work that they did not observe the rising of the fog in time to get away. Doubtless the first thing they saw was an overwhelming force almost over their heads; still I should have thought they would have taken to their boats and risked the chance of being shot in preference to the certainty of a prison.

The thick fog again came on at six, and I left to return to the Admiral. We had three men slightly wounded by shrapnel, but none of any consequence; several balls struck the ship's side, but only those coming through the ports could do much hard at that distance. Poor Mrs Giffard is at Malta with her children. The first lieutenant and surgeon are lately married, but one's sympathies are always more strong for those one knows than for strangers. It is altogether a most sad business, and I don't know when I have passed a more unhappy evening than I did last night. The only consolation is that although we have lost a ship the Russians have not gained one. I suppose they will in the course of time be able to dive for the engine, but it will be none the better for having been in salt water. I suppose experience will make us careful; the "Sidon" and "Niger" but narrowly escaped the "Tiger's" fate, they were neither of them so close to the shore, but both were well within range, and if guns had been brought down in any numbers they must probably have been abandoned. The fogs are wonderfully thick, but still we ought of course to be guided by the lead, and feel our way the more carefully.

Section B: Writing
You are advised to spend about 45 minutes on this section.
You are reminded of the need to plan your answer.
You should write in full sentences.
You should leave enough time to check your work at the end.
(Continue your answer on a separate piece of paper.)

5 'Modern music is rubbish. It sounds awful, the lyrics are terrible, and the performers have no personality.'

Write an article for a broadsheet newspaper in which you explain your point of view about this statement.

(24 marks for content and organisation / 16 marks for technical accuracy.)

These practice papers provide questions on the most popularly studied texts and poems that are common to all exam boards. This means that there may be some sections of this paper that you cannot answer. For these sections, try generating your own questions (as done previously in this workbook) for texts and poems that you have studied. Give yourself the time that is advised on this practice paper and use the mark scheme to help you see how you did.

Practice Paper C GCSE English Literature

Paper 1: Shakespeare and 19th Century Fiction

Time allowed: 1 hour and 45 minutes

Spelling, punctuation and grammar will be assessed in Section A with 4 additional marks available.

Section A: Shakespeare
Answer the question from this section on your chosen text.
(Write your answer on a separate piece of paper.)

Macbeth

Read the following extract from Act 4 Scene 1 and then answer the question that follows. At this point in the play, Macbeth has been presented with visions of the future by the witches. After they vanish, Lennox arrives.

> **LENNOX**   Macduff is fled to England.
>
> **MACBETH**   Fled to England!
> **LENNOX**   Ay, my good lord.
> **MACBETH**   Time, thou anticipatest my dread exploits:
> The flighty purpose never is o'ertook
> Unless the deed go with it; from this moment
> The very firstlings of my heart shall be
> The firstlings of my hand. And even now,
> To crown my thoughts with acts, be it thought and done:
> The castle of Macduff I will surprise;
> Seize upon Fife; give to the edge o' the sword
> His wife, his babes, and all unfortunate souls
> That trace him in his line. No boasting like a fool;
> This deed I'll do before this purpose cool.
> But no more sights!

1 Starting with this speech, explain how far you think Shakespeare presents Macbeth as an evil man. Write about:
  • how Shakespeare presents Macbeth in this speech
  • how Shakespeare presents Macbeth in the play as a whole.   **(30 marks + 4 marks for AO4)**

Romeo and Juliet

Read the following extract from Act 4 Scene 1 and answer the question that follows. At this point in the play, Romeo has been exiled and Juliet has been told she must marry Paris. In desperation, she threatens to kill herself unless the Friar helps her.

JULIET	O shut the door! and when thou hast done so, Come weep with me; past hope, past cure, past help!
FRIAR LAURENCE	Ah, Juliet, I already know thy grief; It strains me past the compass of my wits: I hear thou must, and nothing may prorogue it, On Thursday next be married to this county.
JULIET	Tell me not, friar, that thou hear'st of this, Unless thou tell me how I may prevent it: If, in thy wisdom, thou canst give no help, Do thou but call my resolution wise, And with this knife I'll help it presently. God join'd my heart and Romeo's, thou our hands; And ere this hand, by thee to Romeo seal'd, Shall be the label to another deed, Or my true heart with treacherous revolt Turn to another, this shall slay them both: Therefore, out of thy long-experienced time, Give me some present counsel, or, behold, 'Twixt my extremes and me this bloody knife Shall play the umpire, arbitrating that Which the commission of thy years and art Could to no issue of true honour bring. Be not so long to speak; I long to die, If what thou speak'st speak not of remedy.

2   Starting with this speech, explain how far you think Shakespeare presents Juliet as a strong-willed girl. Write about:
- how Shakespeare presents Juliet in this speech
- how Shakespeare presents Juliet in the play as a whole.

(30 marks + 4 marks for AO4)

The Tempest

Read the following extract from Act 1 Scene 1 and answer the question that follows. At this point in the play, Miranda has been upset by the sight of the shipwreck but Prospero reassures her that all is well.

PROSPERO	Be collected:
	No more amazement: tell your piteous heart
	There's no harm done.
MIRANDA	O, woe the day!
PROSPERO	No harm.
	I have done nothing but in care of thee,
	Of thee, my dear one, thee, my daughter, who
	Art ignorant of what thou art, nought knowing
	Of whence I am, nor that I am more better
	Than Prospero, master of a full poor cell,
	And thy no greater father.
MIRANDA	More to know
	Did never meddle with my thoughts.
PROSPERO	'Tis time
	I should inform thee farther. Lend thy hand,
	And pluck my magic garment from me. So:
	(Lays down his mantle)
	Lie there, my art. Wipe thou thine eyes; have comfort.
	The direful spectacle of the wreck, which touch'd
	The very virtue of compassion in thee,
	I have with such provision in mine art
	So safely ordered that there is no soul –
	No, not so much perdition as an hair
	Betide to any creature in the vessel
	Which thou heard'st cry, which thou saw'st sink. Sit down;
	For thou must now know farther.

3 Starting with this dialogue, explain how far you think Shakespeare presents Prospero as a loving father. Write about:
- how Shakespeare presents Prospero in this dialogue
- how Shakespeare presents Prospero in the play as a whole.   **(30 marks + 4 marks for AO4)**

Section B: 19th Century Fiction

Answer the question from this section on your chosen text.
(Write your answer on a separate piece of paper.)

Great Expectations

Read the following extract from Chapter 2 and then answer the question that follows. In this extract, Dickens introduces the characters of Joe and Mrs Joe.

Joe was a fair man, with curls of flaxen hair on each side of his smooth face, and with eyes of such a very undecided blue that they seemed to have somehow got mixed with their own whites. He was a mild, good-natured, sweet-tempered, easy-going, foolish, dear fellow,—a sort of Hercules in strength, and also in weakness.

My sister, Mrs. Joe, with black hair and eyes, had such a prevailing redness of skin that I sometimes used to wonder whether it was possible she washed herself with a nutmeg-grater instead of soap. She was tall and bony, and almost always wore a coarse apron, fastened over her figure behind with two loops, and having a square impregnable bib in front, that was stuck full of pins and needles. She made it a powerful merit in herself, and a strong reproach against Joe, that she wore this apron so much. Though I really see no reason why she should have worn it at all; or why, if she did wear it at all, she should not have taken it off, every day of her life.

Joe's forge adjoined our house, which was a wooden house, as many of the dwellings in our country were,—most of them, at that time. When I ran home from the churchyard, the forge was shut up, and Joe was sitting alone in the kitchen. Joe and I being fellow-sufferers, and having confidences as such, Joe imparted a confidence to me, the moment I raised the latch of the door and peeped in at him opposite to it, sitting in the chimney corner.

"Mrs. Joe has been out a dozen times, looking for you, Pip. And she's out now, making it a baker's dozen."

"Is she?"

"Yes, Pip," said Joe; "and what's worse, she's got Tickler with her."

At this dismal intelligence, I twisted the only button on my waistcoat round and round, and looked in great depression at the fire. Tickler was a wax-ended piece of cane, worn smooth by collision with my tickled frame.

"She sot down," said Joe, "and she got up, and she made a grab at Tickler, and she rampaged out. That's what she did," said Joe, slowly clearing the fire between the lower bars with the poker, and looking at it; "she Ram-paged out, Pip."

"Has she been gone long, Joe?" I always treated him as a larger species of child, and as no more than my equal.

"Well," said Joe, glancing up at the Dutch clock, "she's been on the rampage, this last spell, about five minutes, Pip. She's a coming! Get behind the door, old chap, and have the jack-towel betwixt you."

---

4 | Starting with this extract, how does Dickens present Joe as a kind but weak character?
Write about:
- how Dickens presents Joe in this extract
- how Dickens presents Joe as a kind but weak man in the novel as a whole. **(30 marks)**

Jane Eyre

Read the following extract from Chapter 7 and then answer the question that follows. In this extract, Jane is a student at Lowood School. Mr Brocklehurst has arrived and ordered that Jane be made to stand on a stool in front of everyone.

"Ladies," said he, turning to his family, "Miss Temple, teachers, and children, you all see this girl?"

Of course they did; for I felt their eyes directed like burning-glasses against my scorched skin.

"You see she is yet young; you observe she possesses the ordinary form of childhood; God has graciously given her the shape that He has given to all of us; no signal deformity points her out as a marked character. Who would think that the Evil One had already found a servant and agent in her? Yet such, I grieve to say, is the case."

A pause—in which I began to steady the palsy of my nerves, and to feel that the Rubicon was passed; and that the trial, no longer to be shirked, must be firmly sustained.

"My dear children," pursued the black marble clergyman, with pathos, "this is a sad, a melancholy occasion; for it becomes my duty to warn you, that this girl, who might be one of God's own lambs, is a little castaway: not a member of the true flock, but evidently an interloper and an alien. You must be on your guard against her; you must shun her example; if necessary, avoid her company, exclude her from your sports, and shut her out from your converse. Teachers, you must watch her: keep your eyes on her movements, weigh well her words, scrutinise her actions, punish her body to save her soul: if, indeed, such salvation be possible, for (my tongue falters while I tell it) this girl, this child, the native of a Christian land, worse than many a little heathen who says its prayers to Brahma and kneels before Juggernaut— this girl is—a liar!"

Now came a pause of ten minutes, during which I, by this time in perfect possession of my wits, observed all the female Brocklehursts produce their pocket-handkerchiefs and apply them to their optics, while the elderly lady swayed herself to and fro, and the two younger ones whispered, "How shocking!" Mr. Brocklehurst resumed.

"This I learned from her benefactress; from the pious and charitable lady who adopted her in her orphan state, reared her as her own daughter, and whose kindness, whose generosity the unhappy girl repaid by an ingratitude so bad, so dreadful, that at last her excellent patroness was obliged to separate her from her own young ones, fearful lest her vicious example should contaminate their purity: she has sent her here to be healed, even as the Jews of old sent their diseased to the troubled pool of Bethesda; and, teachers, superintendent, I beg of you not to allow the waters to stagnate round her."

With this sublime conclusion, Mr. Brocklehurst adjusted the top button of his surtout, muttered something to his family, who rose, bowed to Miss Temple, and then all the great people sailed in state from the room. Turning at the door, my judge said—

"Let her stand half-an-hour longer on that stool, and let no one speak to her during the remainder of the day."

5 | Starting with this extract, how does Brontë make us feel sympathy for Jane?
  Write about:
  ● how Brontë presents Jane in this extract
  ● how Brontë makes us feel sympathy for Jane in the novel as a whole.   **(30 marks)**

Frankenstein

Read the following extract from Chapter 5 and then answer the question that follows. In this extract, Victor Frankenstein has succeeded in bringing the Creature to life.

It was on a dreary night of November that I beheld the accomplishment of my toils. With an anxiety that almost amounted to agony, I collected the instruments of life around me, that I might infuse a spark of being into the lifeless thing that lay at my feet. It was already one in the morning; the rain pattered dismally against the panes, and my candle was nearly burnt out, when, by the glimmer of the half-extinguished light, I saw the dull yellow eye of the creature open; it breathed hard, and a convulsive motion agitated its limbs.

How can I describe my emotions at this catastrophe, or how delineate the wretch whom with such infinite pains and care I had endeavoured to form? His limbs were in proportion, and I had selected his features as beautiful. Beautiful! Great God! His yellow skin scarcely covered the work of muscles and arteries beneath; his hair was of a lustrous black, and flowing; his teeth of a pearly whiteness; but these luxuriances only formed a more horrid contrast with his watery eyes, that seemed almost of the same colour as the dun-white sockets in which they were set, his shrivelled complexion and straight black lips.

The different accidents of life are not so changeable as the feelings of human nature. I had worked hard for nearly two years, for the sole purpose of infusing life into an inanimate body. For this I had deprived myself of rest and health. I had desired it with an ardour that far exceeded moderation; but now that I had finished, the beauty of the dream vanished, and breathless horror and disgust filled my heart. Unable to endure the aspect of the being I had created, I rushed out of the room and continued a long time traversing my bed-chamber, unable to compose my mind to sleep. At length lassitude succeeded to the tumult I had before endured, and I threw myself on the bed in my clothes, endeavouring to seek a few moments of forgetfulness. But it was in vain; I slept, indeed, but I was disturbed by the wildest dreams. I thought I saw Elizabeth, in the bloom of health, walking in the streets of Ingolstadt. Delighted and surprised, I embraced her, but as I imprinted the first kiss on her lips, they became livid with the hue of death; her features appeared to change, and I thought that I held the corpse of my dead mother in my arms; a shroud enveloped her form, and I saw the grave-worms crawling in the folds of the flannel. I started from my sleep with horror; a cold dew covered my forehead, my teeth chattered, and every limb became convulsed; when, by the dim and yellow light of the moon, as it forced its way through the window shutters, I beheld the wretch—the miserable monster whom I had created. He held up the curtain of the bed; and his eyes, if eyes they may be called, were fixed on me. His jaws opened, and he muttered some inarticulate sounds, while a grin wrinkled his cheeks. He might have spoken, but I did not hear; one hand was stretched out, seemingly to detain me, but I escaped and rushed downstairs. I took refuge in the courtyard belonging to the house which I inhabited, where I remained during the rest of the night, walking up and down in the greatest agitation, listening attentively, catching and fearing each sound as if it were to announce the approach of the demoniacal corpse to which I had so miserably given life.

6 Starting with this extract, how does Shelley present Victor Frankenstein's dislike of his creation?
Write about:
- how Shelley presents Victor's reactions to the Creature in this extract.
- how Shelley presents Victor's dislike of the Creature in the novel as a whole. **(30 marks)**

Practice Paper D GCSE English Literature

Paper 2: Modern Texts and Poetry

Time allowed: 2 hours and 15 minutes

Spelling, punctuation and grammar will be assessed in Section A with 4 additional marks available.

Section A: Modern Prose or Drama
Answer one question from this section on your chosen text.
(Write your answer on a separate piece of paper.)

JB Priestley: *An Inspector Calls*

1 How does Priestley present the relationship between the Inspector and Mr Birling?
Write about:
- how the Inspector behaves towards Mr Birling
- how Mr Birling responds to the Inspector.   **(30 marks + 4 marks AO4)**

2 How does Priestley use Shiela to present the theme of guilt?
Write about:
- where Shiela does and doesn't show guilt
- how Priestley presents his ideas in the way that he writes.   **(30 marks + 4 marks AO4)**

Willy Russell: *Blood Brothers*

3 How does Russell use the character of Eddie to explore ideas about class?
Write about:
- how Russell presents Eddie
- how Russell uses these things to explore the theme of class.   **(30 marks + 4 marks AO4)**

4 How does Russell present the theme of depression?
Write about:
- the ideas about depression in the play
- how Russell presents these ideas by the way he writes.   **(30 marks + 4 marks AO4)**

Alan Bennett: *The History Boys*

5 How does Bennett present the relationship between Dakin and Scripps?
Write about:
- the things that Dakin and Scripps discuss
- how Bennett uses these things to show their friendship.   **(30 marks + 4 marks AO4)**

6 How does Bennett explore the theme of reputation?
Write about:
- what different characters say and feel about reputation
- how Bennett uses this to explore ideas about reputation.   **(30 marks + 4 marks AO4)**

William Golding: *Lord Of The Flies*

7 Do you think Simon is an important character in the novel?
Write about:
- how Golding presents the character of Simon
- how Golding uses Simon to present different themes in the novel. **(30 marks + 4 marks AO4)**

8 How does Golding explore the theme of savagery?
Write about:
- which characters display savagery
- how Golding uses this to explore the theme of savagery. **(30 marks + 4 marks AO4)**

George Orwell: *Animal Farm*

9 How does Orwell use Snowball and Napoleon to explore different ideas about leadership?
Write about:
- how Orwell presents Snowball's style of leadership
- how Orwell presents Napoleon's stye of leadership. **(30 marks + 4 marks AO4)**

10 How does the ending summarise the ideas that Orwell is trying to explore in the novel?
Write about:
- how Orwell presents his ideas at the end of the novel
- how Orwell presents these ideas elsewhere in the novel. **(30 marks + 4 marks AO4)**

Kazuo Ishiguro: *Never Let Me Go*

11 How does Ishiguro present the friendship between Kathy and Ruth?
Write about:
- how Ishiguro presents the strengths in their friendship
- how Ishiguro presents the weaknesses in their friendship. **(30 marks + 4 marks AO4)**

12 How does Ishiguro present the theme of nostalgia?
Write about:
- which characters are nostalgic
- how Ishiguro uses this to explore his ideas. **(30 marks + 4 marks AO4)**

Meera Syal: *Anita And Me*

13 How does Syal present the relationship between Meena and her Papa?
Write about:
- how Meena thinks and behaves towards Papa
- how Papa thinks and behaves towards Meena. **(30 marks + 4 marks AO4)**

14 How does Syal present the theme of rebellion?
Write about:
- which characters are rebellious
- how Syal uses this to explore her ideas. **(30 marks + 4 marks AO4)**

Section B: Poetry Anthology
Answer one question from this section.
(Continue your answer on a separate piece of paper.)

Either:

15 **Love and Relationships**

Compare how poets present attitudes towards the opposite sex in 'Sonnet 29 – I Think of Thee' and in one other poem from 'Love and Relationships'. **(30 marks)**

Or:

16 **Conflict and Power**

Compare the ways poets present ideas about war in 'The Charge of the Light Brigade' and in one other poem from 'Conflict and Power'. **(30 marks)**

Section C: Unseen Poetry
Read the two poems below.
Answer both questions in this section.
(Write your answers on a separate piece of paper.)

17 In 'Hawk Roosting', how does the poet present ideas and feelings about hawks? **(24 marks)**

18 In both 'Hawk Roosting' and 'The Owl's Request', the poets convey their ideas and feelings about birds. What are the similarities and differences between the ways the poets present these ideas and feelings? **(8 marks)**

'Hawk Roosting'
by *Ted Hughes*

I sit in the top of the wood, my eyes closed.
Inaction, no falsifying dream
Between my hooked head and hooked feet:
Or in sleep rehearse perfect kills and eat.

The convenience of the high trees!
The air's buoyancy and the sun's ray
Are of advantage to me;
And the earth's face upward for my inspection.

My feet are locked upon the rough bark.
It took the whole of Creation
To produce my foot, my each feather:
Now I hold Creation in my foot

Or fly up, and revolve it all slowly -
I kill where I please because it is all mine.
There is no sophistry in my body:
My manners are tearing off heads -

The allotment of death.
For the one path of my flight is direct
Through the bones of the living.
No arguments assert my right:

The sun is behind me.
Nothing has changed since I began.
My eye has permitted no change.
I am going to keep things like this.

'The Owl's Request'
by *Elizabeth Jennings*

Do not be frightened of me.
I am a night-time creature. When the earth is still,
When trees are shadows of shadows,
When only the moon and its attendant stars
Enlarge the night, when the smallest sound is shrill
And may wake you up and frighten you,
I am about with my friendly, 'Tu-whit, tu whoo'.

My face is kindly but also mysterious.
People call me wise.
Perhaps they do so because I sometimes close my eyes
And seem to be thinking.
The way I think is not like yours. I need
No thick philosopher's book;
I can tell the truth of the world with a look
But I do not speak about
What I see there. Think of me then
As the certainty in your wandering nights.
I can soothe men
And will snatch you out of your doubt,
Bear you away to the stars and the moon
And to sleep and dawn. So lie
And listen to my lullaby.

Answers

PAGES 4–5

1. c, e, f, h
2. 'My mother was rescued from her makeshift tent by a sheep farmer and his wife, grateful patients of my father' / 'She helped around the farm, and cooked and ate the mutton with gratitude'.
3. 1 mark = simple awareness of difference through quotation; 2–3 marks = identifies several differences in own words but writes about father then mother; 4–5 marks = clear understanding of specific differences; 6 marks = full understanding of differences, very well expressed.
4. 1 mark = simple awareness of feelings; 2–3 marks = identifies a few feelings with some quotation as evidence; 4–5 marks = clear understanding of different feelings, with quotations as evidence; 6 marks = full understanding of feelings, well–supported by quotations.
5. 1–2 marks = simple awareness of language and/or structure, with a few references to the text; 3–4 marks = some understanding of how language and/or structure is being used, supported by some quotations; 5–6 marks = clear understanding of how language and structure have been used to achieve some effects, with quotations as evidence; 7–8 marks = full understanding of how language and structure have been used to achieve various effects, well–supported by quotations.

PAGES 6–7

1. a, d, e, g
2. 'It lasts like a family curse' / 'they were haunted; the births, marriages, and deaths associated with the best one was the history of our race for three generations' / 'We were the accessories; we minded them for a little while, and then we passed away. They wore us out and cast us aside.'
3. 1 mark = simple awareness of opinions through quotation; 2 marks = identifies a few thoughts about 'good old things' in own words, but sometimes generalised; 3 = clear understanding of specific thoughts; 4 = full understanding of thoughts, very well expressed.
4. 1 mark = simple awareness of attitudes towards the house; 2–3 marks = identifies a few attitudes with some quotation as evidence; 4–5 marks = clear understanding of different attitudes, with quotations as evidence; 6 marks = full understanding of attitudes, well–supported by quotations.
5. 1–2 marks = simple awareness of language and/or structure, with a few references to the text; 3–4 marks = some understanding of how language and/or structure is being used, supported by some quotations; 5–6 marks = clear understanding of how language and structure have been used to achieve some effects, with quotations as evidence; 7–8 marks = full understanding of how language and structure have been used to achieve various effects, well–supported by quotations.
6. 1–4 marks simple awareness of different feelings, with a few references to the texts; 5–8 marks = identifies several different feelings and tries to compare as well as offer some comments on writers' techniques, supported by some quotations; 9–12 marks = clear understanding and comparison of different feelings and how they are conveyed, with quotations as evidence; 13–16 marks = full comparison of different feelings and the varied ways in which they have been conveyed, well–supported by quotations.

PAGES 8–9

1. b, c, f, g
2. 'low sun was glinting off the brilliant white super yachts' / 'the going was every bit as easy as Kent had promised'.
3. 1 mark = simple awareness of reasons through quotation; 2 marks = identifies a few reasons for setting up the tour in own words, but sometimes generalised; 3 = clear understanding of specific reasons; 4 = full understanding of reasons, very well expressed.
4. 1 mark = simple awareness of attitudes towards the display; 2–3 marks = identifies a few attitudes with some quotation as evidence; 4–5 marks clear understanding of different attitudes, with quotations as evidence; 6 marks = full understanding of attitudes, well–supported by quotations.
5. 1–2 marks = simple awareness of language and/or structure, with a few references to the text; 3–4 marks = some understanding of how language and/or structure is being used, supported by some quotations; 5–6 marks = clear understanding of how language and structure have been used to achieve some effects, with quotations as evidence; 7–8 marks = full understanding of how language and structure have been used to achieve various effects, well–supported by quotations.

PAGES 10–11

1. c, d, e, f
2. 'I have not seen it under very favourable circumstances' / 'when the house is to rights and the furniture all in, I shall be quite sorry to leave it'.
3. 1 mark = simple awareness of setting through quotation; 2 marks = identifies a few points about setting in own words, but sometimes generalised; 3 = clear understanding of specific features of setting; 4 = full understanding of setting, very well expressed.
4. 1 mark = simple awareness of attitudes towards the locals; 2–3 marks = identifies a few attitudes with some quotation as evidence; 3–4 marks = clear understanding of different attitudes, with quotations as evidence; 6 marks = full understanding of attitudes, well–supported by quotations.
5. 1–2 marks = simple awareness of language and/or structure, with a few references to the text; 3–4 marks = some understanding of how language and/or structure is being used, supported by some quotations; 5–6 marks = clear understanding of how language and structure have been used to achieve some effects, with quotations as evidence; 7–8 marks = full understanding of how language and structure have been used to achieve various effects, well–supported by quotations.
6. 1–4 marks simple awareness of different feelings, with a few references to the texts; 5–8 marks = identifies several different feelings and tries to compare as well as offer some comments on writers' techniques, supported by some quotations; 9–12 marks = clear understanding and comparison of different feelings and how they are conveyed, with quotations as evidence; 13–16 marks = full comparison of different feelings and the varied ways in which they have been conveyed, well–supported by quotations.

PAGES 12–13

1. One mark, up to four marks, for each point about the gate–keeper.
2. 1–2 marks = simple awareness of language, with a few references to the text; 3–4 marks = some understanding of how language is being used, supported by some quotations; 5–6 marks = clear understanding of how language has been used to achieve some effects, with quotations as evidence; 7–8 marks = full understanding of how language has been used to achieve various effects, well-supported by quotations.
3. 1–2 marks = simple awareness of narrative structure, such as start or end, with a few references to the text; 3–4 marks = some understanding of the narrative structure and links to audience, supported by some quotations; 5–6 marks = clear understanding of how the narrative structure engages the reader, with quotations as evidence; 7–8 marks = full understanding of how the narrative structure engages the reader, well-supported by quotations.
4. 1–5 marks = simple comments on character, with a few references to the text; 6–10 marks = some evaluative comments about characterisation and writer's techniques, supported by some quotation; 11–15 marks = clear evaluation of characterisation and writer's techniques, with quotations as evidence; 16–20 marks = full evaluation of characterisation and a range of writer's techniques, well-supported by quotations.
5. 1–5 marks simple awareness of characters and feelings, with a few references to the texts;
   6–10 marks = identifies several examples of atmosphere and tries to compare as well as offer some comments on writers' techniques, supported by some quotations; 11–15 marks = clear understanding and comparison of atmosphere and how it is created, with quotations as evidence; 16–20 marks = full comparison of a range of ways in which atmosphere has been created, well-supported by quotations.
6. 1–5 marks simple awareness of settings, with a few references to the texts; 6–10 marks = identifies several examples of setting and tries to compare as well as offer some comments on writers' techniques, supported by some quotations; 11–15 marks = clear understanding and comparison of settings and how they are created, with quotations as evidence; 16–20 marks = full comparison of a range of ways in which settings have been created, well-supported by quotations.

PAGES 14–15

1. One mark, up to four marks, for each point about Ennis.
2. 1–2 marks = simple awareness of language, with a few references to the text; 3–4 marks = some understanding of how language is being used, supported by some quotations; 5–6 marks = clear understanding of how language has been used to achieve some effects, with quotations as evidence; 7–8 marks = full understanding of how language has been used to achieve various effects, well-supported by quotations.
3. 1–2 marks = simple awareness of narrative structure, such as start or end, with a few references to the text; 3–4 marks = some understanding of the narrative structure and links to audience, supported by some quotations; 5–6 marks = clear understanding of how the narrative structure engages the reader, with quotations as evidence; 7–8 marks = full understanding of how the narrative structure engages the reader, well-supported by quotations.
4. 1–5 marks = simple comments on character, with a few references to the text; 6–10 marks = some evaluative comments about characterisation and writer's techniques, supported by some quotation; 11–15 marks = clear evaluation of characterisation and writer's techniques, with quotations as evidence; 16–20 marks = full evaluation of characterisation and a range of writer's techniques, well-supported by quotations.
5. 1–5 marks simple awareness of characters, with a few references to the texts; 6–10 marks = identifies several examples of

characterisation and tries to compare as well as offer some comments on writers' techniques, supported by some quotations; 11–15 marks = clear understanding and comparison of character and how it is created, with quotations as evidence; 16–20 marks = full comparison of a range of ways in which character has been created, well-supported by quotations.
6. 1–5 marks simple awareness of dialogue, with a few references to the texts; 6–10 marks = identifies several examples of dialogue linking to character and/or setting, tries to compare and offer some comments on writers' techniques, supported by some quotations; 11–15 marks = clear understanding of how dialogue conveys character and setting, with quotations as evidence; 16–20 marks = full comparison of a range of ways in which dialogue has been used to convey character and setting, well-supported by quotations.

PAGES 16–17

1. 'In the gloom the courtyard looked of considerable size' or 'I have not yet been able to see it by daylight'.
2. 'I must have been asleep'.
3. 'such a remarkable place' / 'considerable size' / 'great round arches'.
4. The driver doesn't speak to him / The driver seems in a hurry to leave him.
5. 1 mark = simple awareness of setting, with a few references to the text; 2 marks = some understanding of how language is being used, supported by some quotations; 3 marks = clear understanding of how language has been used to achieve some effects, with quotations as evidence; 4 marks = full understanding of how language has been used to achieve various effects, well-supported by quotations.
6. 1 mark = simple awareness of thoughts and feelings, with a few references to the text; 2 marks = some understanding of how language is being used, supported by some quotations; 3 marks = clear understanding of how language has been used to achieve some effects, with quotations as evidence; 4 marks = full understanding of how language has been used to achieve various effects, well-supported by quotations.
7. 1–2 marks = simple awareness of language and/or structure, with a few references to the text; 3–4 marks = some understanding of how language and/or structure is being used, supported by some quotations and evaluative comment; 5–6 marks = clear understanding and evaluation of how language and structure have been used to achieve some effects, with quotations as evidence; 7–8 marks = full evaluative understanding of how language and structure have been used to achieve various effects, well-supported by quotations.
8. 1–2 marks = simple awareness of language and/or structure, with a few references to the text; 3–4 marks = some understanding of how language and/or structure is being used, supported by some quotations and evaluative comment; 5–6 marks = clear understanding and evaluation of how language and structure have been used to achieve some effects, with quotations as evidence; 7–8 marks = full evaluative understanding of how language and structure have been used to achieve various effects, well-supported by quotations.

PAGES 18–19

1. 'And now I come to the point where I met with such sudden and desperate disaster'.
2. 'the rock had been cut away and made top-heavy by the rush of the stream'.
3. 'more amused than alarmed by my adventure' / 'but I had two others in my pocket, so that it was of no importance'.
4. 'I had not told anyone that I proposed to come to the Blue John mine' / 'it was unlikely that a search party would come after me'.

Answers

5. 1 mark = simple awareness of thoughts and feelings, with a few references to the text; 2 marks = some understanding of how language is being used, supported by some quotations; 3 marks = clear understanding of how language has been used to achieve some effects, with quotations as evidence; 4 marks = full understanding of how language has been used to achieve various effects, well-supported by quotations.

6. 1 mark = simple awareness of the mood of hopelessness, with a few references to the text; 2 marks = some understanding of how language is being used, supported by some quotations; 3 marks = clear understanding of how language has been used to achieve some effects, with quotations as evidence; 4 marks = full understanding of how language has been used to achieve various effects, well-supported by quotations.

7. 1–2 marks = simple awareness of language and/or structure, with a few references to the text; 3–4 marks = some understanding of how language and/or structure is being used, supported by some quotations and evaluative comment; 5–6 marks = clear understanding and evaluation of how language and structure have been used to achieve some effects, with quotations as evidence; 7–8 marks = full evaluative understanding of how language and structure have been used to achieve various effects, well-supported by quotations.

8. 1–2 marks = simple awareness of language and/or structure, with a few references to the text; 3–4 marks = some understanding of how language and/or structure is being used, supported by some quotations and evaluative comment; 5–6 marks = clear understanding and evaluation of how language and structure have been used to achieve some effects, with quotations as evidence; 7–8 marks = full evaluative understanding of how language and structure have been used to achieve various effects, well-supported by quotations.

PAGES 20–31

All questions are marked out of 40: 24 marks for content and organisation, and 16 marks for technical accuracy (spelling, punctuation and grammar).

Content and organisation:

1–3 marks = One or two unlinked ideas; no paragraphs; communicates simple meaning; simple vocabulary; occasional sense of purpose, audience and/or form.

4–6 marks = One or two relevant ideas; some attempts to paragraph; communicates simple meanings successfully; simple vocabulary; basic awareness of purpose, audience and form.

7–9 marks = Some linked and relevant ideas; some successful paragraphs; communicates with some success; begins to vary vocabulary and use some linguistic devices; attempts to match purpose, audience and form.

10–12 marks = Increasing variety of linked and relevant ideas; some clear paragraphs; communication is mostly successful; some attempts to make use of vocabulary and linguistic devices; sustained attempt to match purpose, audience and form.

13–15 marks = range of connected and engaging ideas; usually clear paragraphs; communicates clearly; vocabulary and linguistic devices chosen for clear effect; successfully matches purpose, audience and form.

16–18 marks = range of detailed, connected and engaging ideas; clear, useful paragraphs; communication consistently clear and effective; some sophisticated vocabulary and

some range of linguistic devices used effectively; tone, style and register match the purpose, audience and form.

19–21 marks = a range of structured, developed and engaging ideas; consistently effective paragraphing; communication is convincing; sophisticated vocabulary and linguistic devices show evidence of conscious crafting; tone, style, and register consistently match the purpose, audience and form.

22–24 marks = a range of highly structured, developed, complex and engaging ideas; fluently linked paragraphs are used to clarify and emphasise meaning; communication is convincing and compelling; extensive and ambitious vocabulary and linguistic devices show sustained crafting; tone, style, and register are subtly and consistently used to match purpose and form, and to affect the audience.

Technical accuracy (Spelling, Punctuation and Grammar):

1–4 marks = sentences occasionally marked out by full stops; simple range of sentences; occasional Standard English; accurate basic spelling.

5–8 marks = basic sentence structures usually secure; some punctuation within sentences; attempts a variety of sentences; some controlled Standard English; some accurate spelling of more complex words.

9–12 marks = sentences are mostly secure; range of punctuation used, generally with success; uses a variety of sentence forms for effect; mostly Standard English with controlled grammar; generally accurate spelling, including complex and irregular words.

13–16 marks = sentences are consistently secure; wide range of punctuation is used with accuracy; uses a full range of sentence forms for effect; Standard English is consistently used and more complex grammatical structures are used accurately; high level of accuracy in spelling, including ambitious vocabulary.

PAGES 32–33

1. 1 mark for explaining that a simile is a comparison that uses 'like' or 'as'; two further marks for finding an example and explaining the effect of the simile.

2. 1 mark for explaining that a metaphor is a comparison that is written as if it's true (not 'like' or 'as'); two further marks for finding an example and explaining the effect of the metaphor.

3. 1 mark for explaining that personification is describing an object or idea as if it has human qualities; two further marks for finding an example and explaining the effect of the personification.

4. 1 mark for explaining each of the following: alliteration is the repetition of sounds at the start of a series of words, onomatopoeia is words that sound like the sound they describe, and rhyme is when words have the same sound. 6 further marks for finding examples and explaining their effects.

5. 1 mark for each example; 1 mark for explaining the effect created in each example.

All poetry cluster questions are marked out of 15.

1–2 marks = simple comments; one or two direct references to the poem; simple awareness of language.

3–4 marks = relevant comments; direct references to the poem; some reference to techniques of language and/or structure.

5–8 marks = a range of points; some relevant quotations; identification and explanation of some techniques of language and/or structure.

9–11 marks = clear, sustained focus on the question; a range of quotations; understanding of how different techniques of language, structure, and/or form convey meaning.

12–13 marks = thoughtful and developed analysis; a range of well-integrated quotations; sustained analysis of how a variety of different techniques of language, structure and/or form convey meaning.

14–15 marks = exploratory and evaluative analysis; a range of well-integrated quotations; sustained analysis of how a full range of techniques of language, structure, and form convey meaning.

PAGES 34–41

All unseen poetry questions are marked out of 15.

1–2 marks = simple comments; one or two direct references to the poem; simple awareness of language.

3–4 marks = relevant comments; direct references to the poem; some reference to techniques of language and/or structure.

5–8 marks = a range of points; some relevant quotations; identification and explanation of some techniques of language and/or structure.

9–11 marks = clear, sustained focus on the question; a range of quotations; understanding of how different techniques of language, structure and/or form convey meaning.

12–13 marks = thoughtful and developed analysis; a range of well-integrated quotations; sustained analysis of how a variety of different techniques of language, structure and/or form convey meaning.

14–15 marks = exploratory and evaluative analysis; a range of well-integrated quotations; sustained analysis of how a full range of techniques of language, structure and form convey meaning.

PAGES 42–43

All poetry comparison questions are marked out of 30.

1–5 marks = simple comments; awareness of similarity and difference; one or two direct references to the poems; simple awareness of language.

6–10 marks = relevant comments; some comparisons; direct references to the poems; some reference to techniques of language and/or structure.

11–15 marks = a range of points; some focus on comparison; some relevant quotations; identification and explanation of some techniques of language and/or structure.

16–20 marks = clear, sustained focus on the question; clear, sustained comparison; a range of quotations; understanding of how different techniques of language, structure and/or form convey meaning; some consideration of contextual factors.

21–25 marks = thoughtful, developed analysis and comparison; a range of well-integrated quotations; sustained analysis of how a variety of different techniques of language, structure and/or form convey meaning; consideration of contextual factors and alternative interpretations.

26–30 marks = exploratory, evaluative analysis and comparison; a range of well-integrated quotations; sustained analysis of how a full range of techniques of language, structure and form convey meaning; convincing use of contextual factors and alternative interpretations.

PAGES 44–57

All Shakespeare questions are marked out of a total of 30.

1–5 marks = simple comments; one or two direct references to the text; simple awareness of language.

6–10 marks = relevant comments; some focus on the question; direct references to the text; some reference to techniques of language and/or structure.

11–15 marks = a range of points; focus on the question; some relevant quotations; identification and explanation of some techniques of language and/or structure.

16–20 marks = clear, sustained focus on the question; a range of quotations; understanding of how different techniques of language,

structure and/or form convey meaning; some consideration of contextual factors.

21–25 marks = thoughtful and developed analysis; a range of well-integrated quotations; sustained analysis of how a variety of different techniques of language, structure and/or form convey meaning; consideration of contextual factors and alternative interpretations.

26–30 marks = exploratory and evaluative analysis; a range of well-integrated quotations; sustained analysis of how a full range of techniques of language, structure and form convey meaning; convincing use of contextual factors and alternative interpretations.

PAGES 58–63

All 19th Century Fiction questions are marked out of 30 (15 marks for each of the two sections).

1–5 marks = simple comments; one or two direct references to the text; simple awareness of language.

6–10 marks = relevant comments; some focus on the question; direct references to the text; some reference to techniques of language and/or structure.

11–15 marks = a range of points; focus on the question; some relevant quotations; identification and explanation of some techniques of language and/or structure.

16–20 marks = clear, sustained focus on the question; a range of quotations; understanding of how different techniques of language, structure and/or form convey meaning; some consideration of contextual factors.

21–25 marks = thoughtful and developed analysis; a range of well-integrated quotations; sustained analysis of how a variety of different techniques of language, structure and/or form convey meaning; consideration of contextual factors and alternative interpretations.

26–30 marks = exploratory and evaluative analysis; a range of well-integrated quotations; sustained analysis of how a full range of techniques of language, structure and form convey meaning; convincing use of contextual factors and alternative interpretations.

PAGES 64–71

All Modern Fiction questions are marked out of 15

1–2 marks = simple comments; one or two direct references to the text; simple awareness of language.

3–4 marks = relevant comments; some focus on the question; direct references to the text; some reference to techniques of language and/or structure.

5–8 marks = a range of points; focus on the question; some relevant quotations; identification and explanation of some techniques of language and/or structure.

9–11 marks = clear, sustained focus on the question; a range of quotations; understanding of how different techniques of language, structure and/or form convey meaning; some consideration of contextual factors.

12–13 marks = thoughtful and developed analysis; a range of well-integrated quotations; sustained analysis of how a variety of different techniques of language, structure and/or form convey meaning; consideration of contextual factors and alternative interpretations.

14–15 marks = exploratory and evaluative analysis; a range of well-integrated quotations; sustained analysis of how a full range of techniques of language, structure and form convey meaning; convincing use of contextual factors and alternative interpretations.

PAGES 72–74

1. One mark, up to four marks, for each point about the narrator's gratitude.
2. 1–2 marks = simple awareness of language and/or structure, with a few references to the text; 3–4 marks = some understanding of how language and/or structure is being used, supported by some

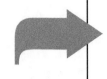

quotations; 5–6 marks = clear understanding of how language and structure have been used to achieve some effects, with quotations as evidence; 7–8 marks = full understanding of how language and structure have been used to achieve various effects, well-supported by quotations.

3. 1–2 marks = simple awareness of narrative structure, such as start or end, with a few references to the text; 3–4 marks = some understanding of the narrative structure and links to audience, supported by some quotations; 5–6 marks = clear understanding of how the narrative structure engages the reader, with quotations as evidence; 7–8 marks = full understanding of how the narrative structure engages the reader, well-supported by quotations.

4. 1–5 marks = simple comments on character, with a few references to the text; 6–10 marks = some evaluative comments about characterisation and writer's techniques, supported by some quotation; 11–15 marks = clear evaluation of characterisation and writer's techniques, with quotations as evidence; 16–20 marks = full evaluation of characterisation and a range of writer's techniques, well-supported by quotations.

5. Content and organisation:

1–3 marks = One or two unlinked ideas; no paragraphs; communicates simple meaning; simple vocabulary; occasional sense of purpose, audience and/or form.

4–6 marks = One or two relevant ideas; some attempts to paragraph; communicates simple meanings successfully; simple vocabulary; basic awareness of purpose, audience and form.

7–9 marks = Some linked and relevant ideas; some successful paragraphs; communicates with some success; begins to vary vocabulary and use some linguistic devices; attempts to match purpose, audience and form.

10–12 marks = Increasing variety of linked and relevant ideas; some clear paragraphs; communication is mostly successful; some attempts to make use of vocabulary and linguistic devices; sustained attempt to match purpose, audience and form.

13–15 marks = range of connected and engaging ideas; usually clear paragraphs; communicates clearly; vocabulary and linguistic devices chosen for clear effect; successfully matches purpose, audience and form.

16–18 marks = range of detailed, connected and engaging ideas; clear, useful paragraphs; communication consistently clear and effective; some sophisticated vocabulary and some range of linguistic devices used effectively; tone, style and register match the purpose, audience and form.

19–21 marks = a range of structured, developed and engaging ideas; consistently effective paragraphing; communication is convincing; sophisticated vocabulary and linguistic devices show evidence of conscious crafting; tone, style, and register consistently match the purpose, audience and form.

22–24 marks = a range of highly structured, developed, complex and engaging ideas; fluently linked paragraphs are used to clarify and emphasise meaning; communication is convincing and compelling; extensive and ambitious vocabulary and linguistic devices show sustained crafting; tone, style, and register are subtly and consistently used to match purpose and form, and to affect the audience.

Technical accuracy (Spelling, Punctuation and Grammar):

1–4 marks = sentences occasionally marked out by full stops; simple range of sentences; occasional Standard English; accurate basic spelling.

5–8 marks = basic sentence structures usually secure; some punctuation within sentences; attempts a variety of sentences; some controlled Standard English; some accurate spelling of more complex words.

9–12 marks = sentences are mostly secure; range of punctuation used, generally with success; uses a variety of sentence forms for effect; mostly Standard English with controlled grammar; generally accurate spelling, including complex and irregular words.

13–16 marks = sentences are consistently secure; wide range of punctuation is used with accuracy; uses a full range of sentence forms for effect; Standard English is consistently used and more complex grammatical structures are used accurately; high level of accuracy in spelling, including ambitious vocabulary.

PAGES 75–78

1. a, c, d, h

2. 1–2 marks = simple awareness of attitudes in both texts with some reference to the texts; 3–4 marks = identifies a few points of comparison, supported by some quotations, but sometimes generalised; 5–6 = clear comparison of attitudes, with quotations; 7–8 = full comparison of attitudes, well-supported by quotations.

3. 1–3 marks = simple awareness of language, with a few references to the text; 4–6 marks = some understanding of how language is being used, supported by some quotations; 7–9 marks = clear understanding of how language has been used to achieve some effects, with quotations as evidence; 10–12 marks = full understanding of how language has been used to achieve various effects, well-supported by quotations.

4. 1–4 marks simple awareness of different attitudes, with a few references to the texts; 5–8 marks = identifies several different attitudes and tries to compare as well as offer some comments on writers' techniques, supported by some quotations; 9–12 marks = clear understanding and comparison of different attitudes and how they are conveyed, with quotations as evidence; 13–16 marks = full comparison of different attitudes and the varied ways in which they have been conveyed, well-supported by quotations.

5. Content and organisation:

1–3 marks = One or two unlinked ideas; no paragraphs; communicates simple meaning; simple vocabulary; occasional sense of purpose, audience and/or form.

4–6 marks = One or two relevant ideas; some attempts to paragraph; communicates simple meanings successfully; simple vocabulary; basic awareness of purpose, audience and form.

7–9 marks = Some linked and relevant ideas; some successful paragraphs; communicates with some success; begins to vary vocabulary and use some linguistic devices; attempts to match purpose, audience and form.

10–12 marks = Increasing variety of linked and relevant ideas; some clear paragraphs; communication is mostly successful; some attempts to make use of vocabulary and linguistic devices; sustained attempt to match purpose, audience and form.

13–15 marks = range of connected and engaging ideas; usually clear paragraphs; communicates clearly; vocabulary and linguistic devices chosen for clear effect; successfully matches purpose, audience and form.

16–18 marks = range of detailed, connected and engaging ideas; clear, useful paragraphs; communication consistently clear and effective; some sophisticated vocabulary and some range of linguistic devices used effectively; tone, style and register match the purpose, audience and form.

19–21 marks = a range of structured, developed and engaging ideas; consistently effective paragraphing; communication is convincing; sophisticated vocabulary and linguistic devices show evidence of conscious crafting; tone, style, and register consistently match the purpose, audience and form.

22–24 marks = a range of highly structured, developed, complex and engaging ideas; fluently linked paragraphs are used to clarify and emphasise meaning; communication is convincing and compelling; extensive and ambitious vocabulary and linguistic devices show sustained crafting; tone, style, and register are subtly and consistently used to match purpose and form, and to affect the audience.

Technical accuracy (Spelling, Punctuation and Grammar):

1–4 marks = sentences occasionally marked out by full stops; simple range of sentences; occasional Standard English; accurate basic spelling.

5–8 marks = basic sentence structures usually secure; some punctuation within sentences; attempts a variety of sentences; some controlled Standard English; some accurate spelling of more complex words.

9–12 marks = sentences are mostly secure; range of punctuation used, generally with success; uses a variety of sentence forms for effect; mostly Standard English with controlled grammar; generally accurate spelling, including complex and irregular words.

13–16 marks = sentences are consistently secure; wide range of punctuation is used with accuracy; uses a full range of sentence forms for effect; Standard English is consistently used and more complex grammatical structures are used accurately; high level of accuracy in spelling, including ambitious vocabulary.

PAGES 79–89

All Shakespeare, 19th Century Fiction and Modern Text questions are marked out of 30.(Questions **1.–14.**)

1–5 marks = simple comments; one or two direct references to the text; simple awareness of language.

6–10 marks = relevant comments; some focus on the question; direct references to the text; some reference to techniques of language and/or structure.

11–15 marks = a range of points; focus on the question; some relevant quotations; identification and explanation of some techniques of language and/or structure.

16–20 marks = clear, sustained focus on the question; a range of quotations; understanding of how different techniques of language, structure and/or form convey meaning; some consideration of contextual factors.

21–25 marks = thoughtful and developed analysis; a range of well-integrated quotations; sustained analysis of how a variety of different techniques of language, structure and/or form convey meaning; consideration of contextual factors and alternative interpretations.

26–30 marks = exploratory and evaluative analysis; a range of well-integrated quotations; sustained analysis of how a full range of techniques of language, structure and form convey meaning; convincing use of contextual factors and alternative interpretations.

Additional spelling, punctuation, and grammar marks for the Shakespeare and Modern Text questions: 1 mark for some accuracy and mostly clear meaning; 2 marks for reasonable accuracy and fully clear meaning; 3 marks for considerable accuracy and written control; 4 marks for consistently accurate and effectively controlled writing.

15.–16. The cluster poetry questions are marked out of 30.

1–5 marks = simple comments; awareness of similarity and difference; one or two direct references to the poems; simple awareness of language.

6–10 marks = relevant comments; some comparisons; direct references to the poems; some reference to techniques of language and/or structure.

11–15 marks = a range of points; some focus on comparison; some relevant quotations; identification and explanation of some techniques of language and/or structure.

16–20 marks = clear, sustained focus on the question; clear, sustained comparison; a range of quotations; understanding of how different techniques of language, structure and/or form convey meaning; some consideration of contextual factors.

21–25 marks = thoughtful, developed analysis and comparison; a range of well-integrated quotations; sustained analysis of how a variety of different techniques of language, structure and/or form convey meaning; consideration of contextual factors and alternative interpretations.

26–30 marks = exploratory, evaluative analysis and comparison; a range of well-integrated quotations; sustained analysis of how a full range of techniques of language, structure and form convey meaning; convincing use of contextual factors and alternative interpretations.

17. The single unseen poetry question is marked out of 24.
1–4 marks = simple comments; one or two direct references to the poem; simple awareness of language.

5–8 marks = relevant comments; direct references to the poem; some reference to techniques of language and/or structure.

9–12 marks = a range of points; some relevant quotations; identification and explanation of some techniques of language and/or structure.

13–16 marks = clear, sustained focus on the question; a range of quotations; understanding of how different techniques of language, structure and/or form convey meaning.

17–20 marks = thoughtful and developed analysis; a range of well-integrated quotations; sustained analysis of how a variety of different techniques of language, structure and/or form convey meaning.

21–24 marks = exploratory and evaluative analysis; a range of well-integrated quotations; sustained analysis of how a full range of techniques of language, structure and form convey meaning.

18. The unseen poetry comparison is marked out of 8.

1–2 marks = simple, relevant comments; some comparisons; direct references to the poems; some reference to techniques of language and/or structure.

3–4 marks = a range of points focussed on the question; clear, sustained comparison; a range of quotations; clear explanation of how different techniques of language, structure and/or form convey meaning.

5–6 marks = thoughtful, developed analysis and comparison; a range of well-integrated quotations; analysis of how different techniques of language, structure and/or form convey meaning.

7–8 marks = exploratory, evaluative comparison; a range of well-integrated quotations; sustained analysis of how a range of techniques of language, structure and form convey meaning.

Acknowledgements

The author and publisher are grateful to the copyright holders for permission to use quoted materials and images.

P.4   From *Auto Da Fay* Reprinted by permission of HarperCollins Publishers Ltd © (HarperCollins) (Fay Weldon).

P.6   From *Thoughts On Cheapness and My Aunt Charlotte* by H G Wells. Reprinted by permission of A P Watt at United Agents on behalf of the Literary Executors of the Estate of H G Wells.

P.8   *'Melbourne in the Moonlight: a nighttime kayak tour'* by Beverley Fearis, Friday 4th April, 2014. Copyright Guardian News & Media Ltd 2014.

P.12   From *The Falls* Reprinted by permission of HarperCollins Publishers Ltd © (Harper Perennial) (Joyce Carol Oates)

P.14   From *Brokeback Mountain*, Reprinted by permission of HarperCollins Publishers Ltd © (Harper Perennial) (Annie Prouxl)

P.34   *Funeral Blues* from From COLLECTED POEMS by W. H. Auden (Vintage, 1991)

P.35   *'Returning We Hear the Larks'* From COLLECTED POEMS by Isaac Rosenberg. Published by Chatto & Windus. Reprinted by permission of The Random House Group Ltd.

P.36   Carol Ann Duffy, 'In Mrs Tilscher's Class' from *The Other Country* (Picador, 2010)

P.37   'The Trees' by Philip Larkin, from *Collected Poems* (Faber and Faber Ltd.)

P.73   From *Unless* Reprinted by permission of HarperCollins Publishers Ltd © (4th Estate, 2010) (Carol Shields)

P.76   Extract from *Who on Earth is Tom Baker?* by Tom Baker, published by Tom Baker Limited © Tom Baker 1997. Reproduced by permission of Sheil Land Associates Ltd.

P.88   'Hawk Roosting' by Ted Hughes, from *Collected Poems* (Faber and Faber Ltd.)

P.88   'The Owl's Request' by Elizabeth Jennings, from *A Spell of Words* (Macmillan, 1997).

P. 24, P.25, P.74 © Neil Kirby
All other images are © Shutterstock.com and © Letts Educational, an imprint of HarperCollins*Publishers* Ltd

Every effort has been made to trace copyright holders and obtain their permission for the use of copyright material. The author and publisher will gladly receive information enabling them to rectify any error or omission in subsequent editions. All facts are correct at time of going to press.

Published by Letts Educational
An imprint of HarperCollins*Publishers*
1 London Bridge Street
London SE1 9GF

ISBN: 9780008318321

Content first published 2015
This edition published 2019

10 9 8 7 6 5 4 3 2 1

Publishing Managers: Rebecca Skinner and Emily Linnett
Commissioning Editor: Katie Galloway
Author: Ian Kirby
Project Management: Sarah Dev-Sherman, Q2A Media
Editorial: Jenny Heath
Cover Design: Sarah Duxbury
Inside Concept Design: Paul Oates
Production: Karen Nulty
Text Design and Layout: Q2A Media
Printed by CPI Group (UK) Ltd, Croydon CR0 4YY

MIX
Paper from
responsible source
FSC
www.fsc.org   FSC™ C007454

This book is produced from independently certified FSC™ paper to ensure responsible forest management.

For more information visit:
www.harpercollins.co.uk/green